MALEDICTA
THE INTERNATIONAL JOURNAL
OF VERBAL AGGRESSION

VOLUME XIII   **1997–2004**

REINHOLD AMAN
EDITOR

MALEDICTA PRESS
P.O. BOX 14123
SANTA ROSA · CA 95402–6123
USA

Library of Congress Catalog
Card Number 77- 649633

ISBN 0–916500–33–0
ISSN 0363–3659

Three out of four doctors recommend Maledicta. The fourth one is a schmuck.

NIHIL + OBSTAT
R 4 July 2005 A

Printed in the United States of America

CONTENTS

VOLUME XIII · 1997–2004

In Memoriam
Spartaco Urbani,
a brilliant, witty, and
much-loved maledictaphile
1919–1992

—*Roberta*

IS THIS THE END OF *MALEDICTA*?
A Maledictorial
Not for the Faint of Heart

Reinhold "Amaretto" Aman

Call me Ishmael. Nah, that's been used. Call me Amaretto, as in "bitter." Indeed, I've grown bitter over the years. And depressed. And all for good reasons: frustrations and disappointments and deaths.

So, Where Have I Been?

Many friends and readers around the world have been wondering whether I'm dead, because they haven't heard from me since 1997. "Are you dead?" is a common question in letters I get. No, I'm not dead yet; I've merely been in a prison again for the past seven years. This time not in a Federal prison but in my own personal prison called "depression," which is far worse than a prison surrounded by razor wire. Depression feels like I'm standing in a deep pit of tar reaching up to my chin and paralyzing me.

Even though I'm a workaholic, I've been feeling helpless, hopeless, and useless since 1997; this forced lethargy was making me very angry. I *wanted* to work but I could not. Doctors tried to turn me into a Happy Zombie with antidepressants, but I know that such pills are just useless Band-Aids covering a deep, incurable wound.

I've tried to figure out the causes of my depression. Some are changes in brain chemistry—the side effects of some blood-pressure and heart medications; others are external—just too many straws on this old camel's back: constructing a big and popular but unprofitable Website, poor book sales, abandoned by my journalist pals, past injustices, the deaths of many friends, and mainly the ever-present dread of having to move again when my current landlord dies, in addition to the realization that *Maledicta* will die the day I die.

The few friends I've told about my clinical depression and the forced move from my Santa Rosa paradise in 2001 reacted in various ways. Some were really helpful: "Stop whining! Knock off your self-pity and *do* something!" Yeah, right. That was as helpful as telling a blind man to do microsurgery. Others told me of *their* problems, illnesses, or deaths in the family. More empathetic friends invited me to spend some time with them in Bangladesh, Japan, Trinidad, Brazil, Holland, Switzerland, and elsewhere, but I can't abandon my feline children; they and *Maledicta* come first.

The reason why I hadn't contacted my subscribers since 1997 is simple: I couldn't afford the printing and mailing of letters. Only those whose e-mail addresses I had knew what was going on.

Tight Bastards

Several years ago, in desperation, I sent an anguished message to *Maledicta* readers, asking them to keep this publication and me alive by contributing a mere $20 (or more if they could afford it) to the Maledicta Survival Fund. Only 8% of those who had bought one or all *Maledicta* volumes and other books responded. Eight friggin' percent. The other 92% ignored my plea or lamented that they couldn't afford to send twenty lousy bucks. They included long-time "fans," well-paid professors whose articles I had painstakingly typeset and published, well-to-do professionals earning $75,000 a year and up, and other tightfisted sons-of-bitches who blow $75 on a restaurant meal or piss away $50 at the bar without batting an eye but who can't afford a small contribution. And you wonder why I'm bitter?

Getting $20 out of the tight fists of a $75,000-to-$100,000-a-year university professor is far more difficult than getting

$50 from a poor widow living on small Social Security checks. That's not hyperbole but a fact.

A Tale of Three Widows

Among the 8% who responded were three widows whose husbands had been genuine fans of this publication. Harriett and Charlene sent checks, but my conscience would not allow me to accept the full amount, knowing of their financial situation. Thus I returned, with a thank-you letter, half of the money donated, because they needed it as much as I did or even more. Returning their checks would have amounted to an insulting rejection of their sincere desire to help.

Then there was Widow No. 3, who sent $20 but who pissed me off with her unjustified whining about the contribution, her being a "poor widow" and all that. Her husband was a great admirer of this journal and even flew to our Maledicta meeting in Houston. He was a high-ranking, very well-paid Texas government official and left her a stately house, a good pension, and plenty of dough—more than enough to allow her to keep buying $100 blouses and $500 dresses. I did not return a cent to that widow but thanked her anyway.

A Tale of Some Pricks

Even though many of my best and most supportive friends are university professors, I have to single out this profession as having the stingiest members imaginable. I'm talking about parsimonious pricks of the first order.

Oh, they **love** *Maledicta.* Such characters tell me how "fascinating" and "fantastic" *Maledicta* is, but most of them are all words and wind. Contributing $20 to keep this unique publication alive? You've got to be kidding. Spending $12.50 to buy a copy? In your dreams, Aman; we're making illegal copies with the department's photocopying machine. This way we won't even have to pay the five-cents-per-page charge at the library's photocopier. *Bastards!*

Oh, don't they **love** *Maledicta*—as long as I keep publishing their articles. Once I decline to do so, because their material is marginal, their tight purse strings get even tighter. No contribution. No more subscription. Hey, no problem. Get lost, you opportunistic cheap-ass bastards!

I have not forgotten the worst of this kind of scholar. I spent uncounted hours correcting his article—fixing up his grammar, style, typos, footnotes, bibliography—and after the volume with his long article appeared, I sent him 10 or 15 free offprints. Then I practically had to *beg* that $75,000-a-year professorial parasite to spend $12.50 to buy a copy of the volume in which his article appeared. *Bastard!*

Am I pissed off at all the tightfisted profs out there? Is the Pope Bavarian?

Based on more than a quarter century of dealing with my readers directly, I have also learned that another group of *Maledicta* "fans" are terribly tight: the rich and super-rich. The richer they are, the tighter. There's only one exception— Steve, a trusting and generous multimillionaire. When I got out of the slammer and was almost broke, he lent me $5,000 so that I could print and mail letters to my subscribers to tell them I was back. Steve also contributed $1,000 when I mailed out the SOS postcards six years later. My kind of guy.

The other rich and super-rich never contributed a dime. I won't mention names, but they were two well-known multi-multimillionaire *Maledicta* "fans" who boasted to their friends how they loved my work; but when asked to contribute just twenty lousy bucks, their enthusiasm evaporated. *Bastards!*

The worst of these—let's call him "Dr. B."—is not only a distant fickle "fan" like the others but visited me twice, driving up in his new Cadillac and wearing $180 running shoes. (Mine cost $16.) When I was on my involuntary Federal Vacation at Terminal Island prison, I was utterly despondent and wrote him a letter begging him to buy the house I was renting, so that my books and the Maledicta Archives would not be tossed if the house were sold while I was in prison.

I explained to him that I would pay the usual rent and that it was a profitable investment, as the local real-estate prices were (and still are) insanely skyrocketing. He could have bought the house for $175,000—peanuts for him. Today the value of that house has increased to some $450,000, not too shabby a gain. But instead, anal-retentive Dr. B. sent me a letter with advice, which I needed like another set of leg irons.

That sumbitch—he's in his eighties—is not just super-rich but filthy-rich: he's worth more than $100 million. His wife hates him. His daughter hates him. His mistress is well taken care of. So what is that old fart going to do with all his money? I don't care, for I will never again lower myself to contact that bastard. *Yemakh shemoy!*

Hey, I'm Not a Bum!

Among those who contributed were 63 who sent $20, of which $15 were meant toward their *Maledicta 13* subscription and the remaining $5 as their contribution. Five bucks. Five bucks? *Five fuckin' bucks!?* After I recovered from the joyous delirium of having received their contribution of five dollars, I felt the sting from what was to me a slap in the face. Hey, I grumbled, either make a contribution of $20 or keep your goddamn money! Five dollars is an insult. True, I am poor, but I still have my dignity and I am not yet a down-and-out bum sitting on the sidewalk and gratefully accepting every dime thrown into the tin cup.

The Internet

The World Wide Web and newsgroups almost killed off *Maledicta*, with my involuntary help. Why buy books when you can get (almost) anything free on the Net? In 1997, around the time my clinical depression began, I discovered the Internet—fortunately and unfortunately.

Fortunately, because I could evade depressing reality by reading news from every corner of the world—from Bavarian newspapers to Brazilian weeklies; by mining the treasure trove of information about *everything*—from Albanian dialects to Zulu grammars; and by participating in language-oriented newsgroups—teaching, entertaining, or viciously fighting the kooks, morons, assholes, and nasties who infest such groups.

Unfortunately, because I wasted about seven years engaging in nonproductive nonsense on the Net, unable to concentrate on *Maledicta*, and waiting for the sword of Damocles to drop. It finally dropped in 2001, when my dear old landlady Hazel died and her heirs sold the house, forcing me to find another *ersatz* paradise. After six months of looking for a simple house and a landlord who would accept some of my cats, I found such a place seven miles south of Santa Rosa, in rural Cotati. With the financial and muscular help of my daughter Susan and her husband Rob and two young Mexican friends, we moved my books and stuff to my current place.

Tacky Ticker

Still in the grip of depression, still screwing around the Internet, and *Maledicta 13* still far from being finished, I had another heart attack, followed by open-heart surgery with triple bypass. Just what I needed. A month later, one bypass closed up, causing yet another heart attack. *Shit! Fuck! Piss!* Could anything *else* go wrong? Sho' 'nuff—the murderous cluster headaches started their unpredictable cycle and drove me very close to you-know-what. But after several week-long cycles (and two decades of those horrible headaches), I finally found pills to stop these devastating and incapacitating attacks. And best of all, I finally was able to drag myself out of that tar pit.

In December 2004, I quit all time-wasting newsgroups cold turkey, which, if you are familiar with such a tar baby, is as difficult as quitting cigarets or booze or hard drugs. I began using my time to finish this volume, whipping out a few articles, and going over the earlier typeset pieces for final typographical embellishments. Then I started to plan the shipping of *Maledicta 13*, which has become a nightmare. Gone are the days of dividing the shipping cartons into three groups: USA, Canada, elsewhere. Now all books shipped to foreign countries have to be assigned to one of five world regions; damned customs forms have to be filled out for every book; and the insanely high postage rates have to be calculated for each country on my list of subscribers. All these chickenshit chores are enough to cause permanent erectile dysfunction.

Dying Friends

In addition to the frustrations and disappointments mentioned, the deaths of many friends—human and feline—were getting me deeper into that tar pit of depression. Many friends and acquaintances, both local unknowns and world-famous ones, have died in the past years. My landlady's slow death, my friend Richard's slow decline from prostate cancer, the sudden death from pancreatic cancer of a young pen pal in Canada, and the painful death of my sweet cat "Smokie" affected me deeply. The deaths of other, well-known friends and true *Maledicta* fans kept me in that tar pit: gone forever are Allen Walker Read, Elias Petropoulos, Ernest Borneman, Gershon Legman, David Ludwig Bloch, Franz Kiener, Morrie Camhi, Lou Harrison, Harry Zohn, Scott Beach, Don Laycock, Stanley Kubrick, Leslie Charteris, Frank Muir, Leon Uris, Freddy Heineken, Joel Oppenheimer, and dozens more ... one after the other. Every time a human or feline friend dies, a part of me dies.

Poor but Proud

I am poor—by choice—and don't mind it. Had I remained in the petroleum-chemistry field, I'd now be living in my own house somewhere in Southern California, with a fat pension, a big monthly Social Security check, and not having to think twice about whether a restaurant charges $5 or $25 for a plate of spaghetti and meatballs. But I chose a different path by dedicating my life to languages and *Maledicta*. A comfortable old age be damned.

As a result of my choice, I've been living in genteel poverty ever since "Judge" Becker, that stupid, paranoid, nasty cunt, robbed me of some $90,000 in my 1990 divorce. (She's already burning in deepest Hell.) I've always lived a simple, almost ascetic life. Fancy clothes and gourmet food mean nothing to me. I'm not interested in partying, boozing or drugs. As long as I have a dry roof over my head, enough money to feed my pets, and the funds to publish *Maledicta*, I'm happy. Fortunately, I have no money-wasting vices: No traveling. No golfing. No hunting. No fishing. No women. No sheep.

Food is for me just fuel to keep the body going. I spend an average of $1.25 a day on food and enjoy such simple meals as a plate of ramen noodles; that's ten cents for a stomach-filling supper. Or, a can of beef stew (89¢ on sale). I'm telling you this only to let you know that I don't waste any financial contributions but use them wisely to keep *Maledicta* and *moi* alive. No lying and laying on nearby California beaches. No blowing your bucks on big-busted bimbos. All goes to keep *Maledicta* alive.

As can be expected—judging from experience—there will be a few snotty or smart-ass jerks and jerkettes who'll accuse me of whining and wallowing in self-pity. As we philologists are wont to say: they can go fuck themselves. I'm merely reporting the facts. Those who are annoyed by my honesty, openness, and factual statements don't have to inform me; they should just *shove* their sniping and beat it.

There are of course hundreds of other dedicated one-man and one-woman publishers in the same situation as I am. They, too, struggle every day with the disappointments and frustrations that are part of putting out a publication without the support of a mainstream or university teat. But whereas many other micro-publishers put on a happy face for fear of alienating their sensitive readers and losing subscribers, I have never played this game.

A Businessman I Am Not

The worst financial mistake I've made as publisher was shipping *Maledicta 12* gratis to all who had prepaid *Maledicta 11*. Being an immaculately scrupulous ex-con, I decided to give away the 160-page *Maledicta 12* in order to keep my implied promise to them of delivering 320 pages for the money they had paid. I absorbed all expenses of printing and shipping that volume to prove that I was still an honest fellow, even though I had become a jolly good felon.

For this act of kindness—or rather, utter economic and unbusinessmanlike stupidity—I expected my "fans" to subscribe to *Maledicta 13*. Only about 285 did; the others, including long-time subscribers and authors whose stuff I had published, as well as librarians, just said, "Thank you, sucker. Good-bye." No subscriptions, not one cent when I sent out the desperate SOS postcards for contributions to the Maledicta Survival Fund. Heartless bastards! Niggardly, anal-retentive sumbitches!

I'm still selling *Maledicta* and other books at 1970s prices or lower, despite the inflation during the past 30 years and seeing my books huckstered by greedy American, British, and Canadian used-book-peddling vultures for up to $100.

Cacademic journals are extremely pricey: the equivalent of 160 pages of *Maledicta* cost between $75 and $120. Have a look at the incredible prices charged for John Benjamins journals or the books published by de Gruyter, Niemayer, or Elsevier. Yet I, Mr. Time Warp, have been selling *Maledicta* at 1970s prices for $12.50 or less per 160 pages. Those other publications have a captive audience, though: college and university libraries, which are forced to subscribe to such overpriced journals by professors who are too damn cheap to subscribe to their professional publications.

However, reality now forces me to finally raise the price for *Maledicta* a bit, to $20.00, which is still way underpriced considering its uniqueness and quality.

A Tale of Two Subscribers; Or, How to Die Young

In 1978, I offered low-priced two-year and five-year subscriptions to *Maledicta*, to raise the funds needed to buy the IBM Selectric Composer with which I typeset volumes I to V. One reader in San Diego wrote that he didn't want to pay in advance for two years. "You could die before the second volume appears, and I'd be out $15." So he subscribed for only one year at the regular rate.

Then there was an optimistic 82-year-old gentleman in San Francisco who subscribed for five years. Not only did he live long enough to get all five volumes, but he enjoyed two more years before going to The Big Maledicktor Up There.

Oh, yes: The financial worrywart from San Diego died after getting his one-year subscription. The moral: Don't worry about losing a few bucks or you'll die before your time.

~

Despite the many unpublished articles and stacks of clippings I have for further volumes, I'm afraid this will be the end of *Maledicta*—unless a fat-cat supporter sponsors the next volume or more readers contribute to keep it alive, especially the 92% who so far have never sent a dime. I went deep into debt (some $10,000) to produce, print, and ship this volume. My credit cards are maxed out.

By presenting this report I'm not asking for your sympathy. It should also not be misconstrued as "whining." Whining is for wimps. I *bitch*, because there's so much to bitch about.

Finally, let me ask you: if *you* had to choose between (1) swallowing your pride by having to ask your readers to help out financially and (2) jumping off the Golden Gate Bridge to become fish food, what would *you* do?

"PLEASE DELETE THE FOLLOWING..."
Censoring a Saturday Morning Cartoon Show

Ken Pontac

O ne of the first justifications of the censor is, "We must protect the children!", a ploy meant to strike deeply into the maternal and paternal instincts of the public. Since children are apparently too stupid to understand the difference between fantasy and reality, and their parents are obviously not to be trusted with overseeing the children's viewing habits, it has become the sacred mission of the censor to decide what is fit for public consumption. Nowhere is this reasoning more prevalent than in the abyss of Saturday morning cartoons. As a producer of an animated television show for Saturday morning broadcast, I get many letters from the censor (Broadcast Standards & Practices, or "BS&P") about the content of my show. The deleterious content includes:

- ▶ acts of interpersonal violence
- ▶ dangerous and imitable actions
- ▶ tastefulness (or lack thereof)
- ▶ adult sexual humor
- ▶ offensive or ridiculing references
- ▶ sarcasm

Following below are examples of the hundreds of warnings I have received from this august body over a two-year period. My comments are in *italics*.

Acts of Interpersonal Violence
Please insure that the action in which the character's limbs are tied into knots does not appear as painful.

Please delete the steam coming from the boiling lobster pot.

Please insure that the grabbing of the chicken's neck should not appear as a choke.

Please ensure that the Storyboard artist equips the character with a table knife, since he is merely preparing to eat lunch, rather than a knife which would play as a lethal weapon. Thanks.

Dangerous and Imitable Actions

As agreed, the car will accelerate into flight so that it is actually flying through the air by the time it approaches the wall. This bit of action distances the stunt from the real-life world of children's play, where the laws of physics must apply, thereby (we hope) reducing the likelihood of a child's trying to drive his Big Wheel through the wall.

The term "as agreed" is a trick of the censor when leaving a paper trail; there is generally no previous "agreement" in these instances.

As agreed, please lose the character's action of smashing through walls. This action is dangerous and imitable.

Please avoid references to a game entitled "Suicide Roller Skate Death." Also, do not discuss the normal outcome of this game as being a trip through the washing machine rinse cycle. Substitute something which is not potentially dangerous, imitable or attractive.

Tastefulness

Caution on the appearance of the "snot." As agreed at Script stage, we expect this to look clear and shiny rather than thick, green and disgusting. As you know, any depiction of nasal mucus brings with it questions of good/bad taste as well as problems for our Sales division. Please ensure that what is shot is not overly graphic.

A common BS&P tactic is to invoke the specter of Sales Problems, since any Network arbitrator will favor commerce over art if a tie-breaking decision is needed.

Please delete the action of the character "letting one fly." While a "burp," indicating stomach gas, would be allowable, lower intestinal flatulence is unacceptable.

The rules never stay the same with BS&P. Some time after this memo regarding the "allowability" of burping, I received the following:

Because of the rude, antisocial aspects of belching, we need to avoid our character's belching unless comment is made about the behavior being inappropriate. Parents and teachers will not appreciate our series undermining their legitimate attempts to teach children what is—and is not—acceptable behavior. Thus, please lose both of these "belches" or keep one, adding a line of reprimand regarding the belch, and substitute for the second.

Kindly tone down the exceedingly prolonged and disgusting "burp" at the end of the song. With six "burps" SFX already within the lyrics of this particular song, we are pushing the limits of broadcast acceptability. The final "belch" SFX is a Sales problem even in an experimental series such as this. Thank you.

Please lose: "Hold your water."

Please do not use the alternate line: "...his booger box gets bigger." I agreed to only one reference to nasal mucus as "boogers" and that line occurred on page 7.

Please substitute for "stinkpot" as it is a vulgarity. Thanks!

According to BS&P, "stinkpot" is a slang term for vagina. I have looked in many slang dictionaries and have been unable to verify this definition.

We are evaluating the line: "Get bent" to determine if the expression has a hidden slang meaning that would not be acceptable for Saturday morning broadcast.

We are researching the term "Hour of the Antelope" and will get back to you.

The regurgitation of the map must be handled in good taste. I would suggest a cough or hiccup rather than a belch or vomit action. Can we discuss? Also, caution that the map is not covered with stomach contents or secretions.

Adult Sexual Humor

As agreed at Script level, please delete the word "masticated" from the line. As an unfamiliar word referring to something which happens inside the closet, it will play as "masturbated." Let's discuss.

Please do not use the following pictures: "The Birth of Venus" and "Christina's World" as both of these pictures contain nude women.

Christina's World contains no nude women.

The cocktail sausage line plays as adult sexual humor. Please substitute acceptably.

Please substitute for the underlined language: "Get off my green butt" and "Zip your lip, dirt bag!" These expressions are either overly crude for Saturday morning broadcast or have adult sexual connotation.

Also, caution on the expression, "Torque my cork." Is there any way we can play this line, perhaps with a gesture towards the character's head, so as to ensure that this line is not interpreted as a penis reference?

As agreed, "Then I say we BLOW UP your clothes!" will be replaced with "Then I say we DISINTEGRATE your clothes!"

Offensive or Ridiculing References

Kindly substitute for the expression "What a gyp!" The word "gyp" is short for "gypsy." In the context of theft or cheating, it perpetuates negative stereotypes about persons of Romany descent.

Kindly substitute for the joke: "I feel a severe case of narcolepsy coming on." We do not permit humor at the expense of disabled or medically compromised persons.

Please delete the unscripted: "And you thought ebola was tough to shake." We wish to avoid ridicule of those with the deadly ebola virus.

Kindly remove the logo "For a Chil'n" from the huge jar of baby food. The expression "Chil'n" is Black dialect, and may be interpreted as negative racial comment.

Please lose the reference to "bingeing and purging." We do not wish to indulge in humor at the expense of people with the very real problems of anorexia and bulimia.

Please delete the phrase: "You're so stupid!" We wish to avoid negative IQ references.

Please substitute for the underlined: "I'm a trained idiot."

Please delete the word "mad." We do not wish to ridicule people with mental health disorders.

As agreed, "I have gone blind!" will be replaced with "I can't see!"

Please lose the "three-legged dogs" lines. This plays as an in-breeding joke and is inappropriate for Saturday morning.

I suppose this might be offensive to those viewers living in Appalachia.

Thanks for agreeing to lose the cracks about Kosher ham and Union grapes.

As agreed, the line: "Cattle mutilations and stuff, of course," will be cut due to the many animal activist organizations.

Please delete all "Voodoo" references and the term "Voodoo Queen."

Please delete the "weird chant." This type of material connotes occult rites and is of concern to many of our viewers.

Please substitute for the remark from character when the acid passes through his hands: "Stigmata! How divine!"

Please delete the Indian head from the station test pattern. We do not wish to ridicule American Indians.

Please delete the reference to President Kennedy's assassination date. This is not an appropriate vehicle for humor.

[Regarding] pages 30, 31, 32, 34: There are numerous "blind jokes" in these scenes. We do not wish to ridicule those whose vision is seriously impaired.

In phone conversations with BS&P about the "blind" character we were told, "She's very, very funny to us, and that's the problem." The BS&P solution to this problem was, "If you take the humor away, it will work for me." We were attempting to make a funny cartoon, but the quality of the show is never the issue with BS&P.

Please substitute for the line: "This sort of thing has to be done just right. Otherwise you could get a crippling spinal cord injury and be involved in an expensive and time consuming lawsuit."

Regardless of what the to-be-agreed-upon attack consists of, it will not be acceptable to have this battle punctuate the cherished Christmas hymn "Silent Night." The latter contains a great deal of religious content. Thus, the scripted parody of battle over phrases such as "Holy infant, so tender and mild" is certain to offend many of our viewers.

Sarcasm

Please substitute for the cynical remark about Christmas as being indestructible because "It's too big, too marketable."

The line: "It goes to show that violence is never the answer" plays as sarcastic and must be deleted for Saturday morning broadcast.

Please modify character's line: "Contrary to popular opinion, Saturday morning cartoons aren't comprised solely of base humor and glorified violence." We are concerned with the sarcasm of this line and the statement is a direct put-down of our own product.

As agreed, the sarcastic: "That was the moral, kids, in case any of you didn't catch it," will be replaced with "Darn."

JOE ZEUGMA LIMERICKS

Hugh Clary

Joe Zeugma could not get a date,
Which left him a piteous state,
But with help from his name
He finally came
Into money, her bedroom, and Kate.

Though the flu had Joe Zeugma's new miss,
She unselfishly offered him bliss;
On her way to Peru,
She stopped and she blew
His dick, and her nose, and a kiss.

Joe Zeugma was feeling no pain,
Which his fortunes today would explain:
After doing his best
On his algebra test,
Scored an "A", then some dope, and with Jane.

Though she cooked all her meals hard as rocks,
Joe Zeugma's new girl was a fox,
So when offered a plate,
He triumphantly ate
Humble pie, like a pig, and her box.

Joe Zeugma loves girls that are quick,
Like Betty, a dexterous chick,
Who makes breakfast, completing
Her chores, while she's beating
The clock, scrambled eggs, and his dick.

It's the morning right after the race,
And Joe Zeugma has smiles on his face;
Life's all that he dreamed
Cuz he mightily creamed
His rivals, his tea, and in Grace.

When Joe Zeugma sees nuns in their eighties,
He streaks like a fiend out of Hades
 And, batting his lashes,
 He suddenly flashes
His lantern, a smile, and the ladies.

Joe Zeugma had just shot his rocks,
When he noticed the sign that read, "Pox
 Has infected this sheep,"
 And found himself deep
In trouble, and thought, and its box.

Joe Zeugma's new girl, Nancy Todd,
Likes basketball, dice, and his bod,
 So each weekend's a hoot
 When he's able to shoot
Some craps, and some hoops, and his wad.

While prospecting, buxom Miss Jones
Struck gold, where Joe Zeugma found stones.
 So, never a grump,
 He decided to jump
For joy, and her claim, and her bones.

To Proud Mary Joe Zeugma once showed
That in semen are vitamins stowed
 In hopes she would follow
 The logic and swallow
The bait, and her pride, and his load.

Joe Zeugma, when landing with clatter,
Confessed he was wiser but sadder:
 In attempting, coition-ly,
 The position of Titian, he
Fell from grace, and from Grace, and the ladder.

Joe Zeugma's vexations are myriad,
Since his girlfriend, a cutie named Kiryad,
 Has gotten him pissed
 By saying she missed
The bus, a day's work, and her period.

HOW BULGARIANS
RELIEVE THEIR SOULS

Vladimir I. Zhelvis

It is not surprising that Bulgarians, so close to Russians in culture, turn in anger to their variation of the notorious Russian *mat*. One of the strongest curses is **Da ti eba maikata!** ("I fuck your mother!") If you utter it in a public place, you may end up in court.

If a Bulgarian wants to tell you that you'd better take off, or else, he will say, perhaps, **Ebi si maikata!** ("Go fuck your mother!") This is not the only obscene way to vilify a mother. Exceptionally obscene is the promise **Turyam (or hakam) go na maikati!** (lit., "I'll stick him in the mother!" implying, "I'll stick my prick in your mother's mouth!") A special abusive intonation is needed here. **Turyam (or hakam) go (khuya) na maika ti v geza!** ("I'll stick him [my prick] in your mother's ass!") is similar. My informant added here that in such curses old Oriental tastes might find expression.

When a Bulgarian has nobody but himself to blame for a misfortune, for example, when he is late for his train, he may exclaim indignantly, **Gore (or okh) da si eba maikata!** ("Oh, fuck your mother!") This is not a very common curse.

Many strong insults are used against women. **Kurva** ("whore") is considered extremely obscene and is strictly taboo in public places. Of almost the same meaning is **maetiya** ("a bitch in heat").

Men are not ignored either. **Putko** and **putka**, lit. "aunt," are applied exclusively to the stronger half of humanity. Special intonation is needed. Also **piderast** ("pederast; homosexual") is quite bad. If you use it openly, you may find yourself in court facing a severe penalty.

An extremely nasty term is **kopele** ("bastard"), especially when hurled at children. My informant advised me never to use it. Of similar force is **izrod** ("monster"), referring to physical deformity.

Some derogatory vocatives may be used in a very friendly way, as an intimate address. Such is **khuyu** ("prick"), just a joking vocative among young males. **Idiot** ("idiot") and **govedo** ("cattle") are quite strong, but in a friendly circle they do not sound too offensive.

Among other less shocking invectives are **levak**, an awkward man who is not very competent with the other sex, and **selyanin** ("churl, country guy"), an uncouth, ill-bred person. **Zandana** is untranslatable; it is applied to a person who is filthy in spirit, dishonest and disgusting. **Kuchi sun** ("son of a dog") is very close to English *son-of-a-bitch*.

On the whole, Bulgarians use their Dirty Dozen rather freely and evidently find it a useful tool in their fight with the adversities of life.

Copyright © 1996 by Andy Singer

EXPENSIVE *ARSCHLOCH*
German Traffic Fines

Reinhold Aman

In Germany, insults aimed by drivers at police officers and meter maids (*Politessen*) are heavily fined. The amount of the fine depends on the circumstances and especially on the income of the offender. Normally, the fine is 10 to 30 *Tagessätze* (a *Tagessatz* is ⅓₀ of one's monthly net income), but judges are free to vary the amounts shown below.

For example, Stefan Effenberg, a wealthy German ex-soccer star, was stopped on 19 February 2003 for speeding on the Autobahn A2 near Braunschweig. He called the police officer "**Arschloch**" (asshole). A judge fined him 100,000 Euro (20 *Tagessätze* at each 5,000 Euro), later reduced to 90,000, about US$117,000. Effenberg claimed that he had only said to the cop "Schönen Abend noch!" (Have a nice evening). [*Bild-Zeitung*, 4 Nov. 2004; *Der Standard* (Austria), 28 April 2005]

Some of the English translations of the following German insults are only approximations. Currently, one Euro equals around US$1.30.

Fines for Insulting a Meter Maid

Dumme Kuh (stupid cow): 300–800 Euro
Du Schlampe (You slut): 1,900 Euro
Fieses Miststück (ugly bitch): 2,500 Euro
Alte Sau (old pig): 2,500 Euro
Habt ihr blöden Weiber nichts Besseres zu tun? (Don't you stupid/silly broads have anything better to do?): 500 Euro
Zu dumm zum Schreiben ([You're] too stupid to write): 450 Euro

Fines for Insulting a Police Officer

Du (thou; i.e., using the familiar address): 600 Euro
Depp (dope, idiot): 200–450 Euro
Witzbold (joker) or **Bekloppter** (nut): 200–600 Euro
Asozialer (asocial one): 550 Euro
Sie Holzkopf (You wooden head): 750 Euro

Wichtelmann (dwarf, runt): 1,000 Euro
Du Wichser (You jerk-off, masturbator): 1,000 Euro
Raubritter (robber baron): 1,500 Euro
Trottel in Uniform (moron wearing a uniform): 1,500 Euro
Wegelagerer (highwayman): 450 Euro
Am liebsten würde ich jetzt Arschloch zu Ihnen sagen (I'd really
  like to call you an asshole): 1,600 Euro
Leck mich doch (Why don't you kiss/lick [my ass]): 300 Euro
Was willst du, du Vogel? (What do you want, bird?): 500 Euro
Ihnen hat wohl die Sonne das Gehirn verbrannt? (Did the sun
  burn/fry your brain?): 600 Euro
An insult plus a slap in the face: 6,000 Euro

Gestures

▸ Sticking out tongue at an officer: 150 Euro
▸ Making a circle with thumb and index finger (*Arschloch!* = asshole!): 675–750 Euro
▸ Repeatedly hitting the index finder at one's temple or forehead
  (*den Vogel zeigen*, lit. 'to show the bird' meaning "You're nuts"):
  750–1,000 Euro
▸ Giving the finger (called *Stinkefinger* "stink-finger" in German):
  depending on city and rank of the police officer: up to 4,000 Euro

Source: ADAC *(German Automobile Club)*

DEPRESSED?
OVERWORKED?
JOB SUCKS?
UNAPPRECIATED?
FAMILY PROBLEMS?
MONEY WORRIES?
Have *we* got a pill for you!

| **F U K I T O L** | 1000 mg |

When Life Just Sucks ... **FUKITOL!**

HOW TO DECIPHER PERSONALS ADS

WOMEN'S ADS

40-ish	49
Adventurous	Slept with everybody
Athletic	No tits
Average looking	Has a face like a basset hound
Contagious smile	Does a lot of pills
Educated	Banged her Political Science professor
Emotionally secure	Medicated
Feminist	Fat ball-buster
Free spirit	Junkie
Friendship first	Former slut
Fun	Annoying
Gentle	Comatose
Good listener	Borderline autistic
New-Age	All body hair, all the time
Old-fashioned	Lights out, missionary position only, no blowjobs
Open-minded	Desperate
Outgoing	Loud and embarrassing
Passionate	Sloppy drunk
Poet	Depressive schizophrenic
Professional	Certified bitch
Redhead	Bad dye-job
Romantic	Looks better by candle light
Rubenesque	Grossly fat
Social	Has been passed around like an hors d'oeuvre tray
Voluptuous	Very fat
Wants soul mate	Stalker
Weight proportional with height	Hugely fat
Widow	Drove first husband to kill himself
Young at heart	Old bat

MEN'S ADS

40-ish	52 and looking for 25-year-old
Athletic	Watches a lot of NASCAR
Average looking	Unusual hair growth on ears, nose, back
Educated	Will patronize the shit out of you
Free spirit	Banging your sister
Friendship first	As long as friendship involves sex

Fun	Good with a remote and a six pack
Good-looking	Arrogant
Very good-looking	Dumb as a board
Honest	Pathological liar
Huggable	Overweight; more body hair than a bear
Likes to cuddle	Insecure mama's boy
Mature	Older than your father
Open-minded	Wants to sleep with your roommate
Physically fit	Does a lot of 12-ounce curls
Poet	Wrote ex-girlfriend's phone number on a bathroom stall
Sensitive	Cries at chick flicks
Very sensitive	Gay
Spiritual	Got laid in a cemetery once
Stable	Arrested for stalking but not convicted
Thoughtful	Says "Excuse me" when he farts

WOMEN'S ENGLISH

Yes = No
No = Yes
Maybe = No
We need = I want
I'm sorry = You'll be sorry
We need to talk = You're in trouble
Sure, go ahead = You better not
Do what you want = You'll pay for this later
I'm not upset = Of course I'm upset, you moron!
You're certainly attentive tonight = Is sex all you ever think about?

MEN'S ENGLISH

I'm hungry = I'm hungry
I'm sleepy = I'm sleepy
I'm tired = I'm tired
Nice dress = Nice cleavage
I love you = Let's have sex now
I'm bored = Do you want to have sex?
May I have this dance? = I'd like to have sex with you.
Can I call you sometime? = I'd like to have sex with you.
Do you want to go to a movie? = I'd like to have sex with you.
Can I take you out to dinner? = I'd like to have sex with you.
I don't think those shoes go with that outfit = I'm gay.

Thanks to Lewis T., Pete Metzger, David Pressman, Lou Boxer *et al.*

SOME TERMS FOR WOMEN AT AN AUSTRALIAN MILITARY ACADEMY

Bruce Moore

This article documents some terms used by cadets at the Royal Military College, Duntroon, Australia (hereafter abbreviated to Duntroon), to describe women in the period 1983–85. Most of the terms are pejorative, and the reasons for this insistent pejoration are canvassed in the course of the article. The article concludes with a word list of the terms which were in use during this period. Although some of the terms were used by all cadets, it is not suggested that all the terms were in common use (nor is it suggested that these are the *only* pejorative terms for women which were used by cadets—it is likely that many common terms from the area of general Australian slang were not listed or mentioned by respondents). What the study reveals is a system which encodes such attitudes towards women as are common in the wider community, and yet especially intense and insistent within a special social environment.

From 1911 to 1985 Duntroon was Australia's prestige institution for the training of male officers for the Australian Army. In addition to their military training cadets had always received some academic training, and by 1968 this had become formalized by means of an association with one of Australia's major universities. Within Duntroon there was created a Faculty of Military Studies, and this Faculty was part of the autonomous University of New South Wales. Cadets were required to gain a degree in Arts, Science, or Engineering, and after completing this traditional university work, they did a further year of military studies. In the early 1980s, however, the Australian Government decided to create a new institution, the Australian Defence Force Academy, which would train both male and female officers for the three services—army, navy, and air force. This new institution began operations in 1986.

It had long been recognized that Duntroon cadets had developed their own special "slang" system,[1] and it was clear that the changeover to the new institution would either destroy or at least radically alter that system. In the light of this the English Department of the Royal Military College decided to survey the lexical habits of cadets in the 1983–85 period—partly for the purpose of historical recording, and partly to provide a body of evidence which could be compared with the language of cadets at the new institution at a later date. The survey took the form of questionnaires and interviews. This article deals with one area of lexical density in the slang system of Duntroon cadets.

The College is located in Canberra, the capital of Australia, a city of about 250,000 people. Cadets were not isolated from the Canberra community: they made full use of the city's cultural, recreational, and sporting facilities. Nevertheless, there were forces at work which served to isolate the cadets from that wider community in quite important ways. For most of the time the cadets were working together in a military environment, and their days were rigidly timetabled with military and academic requirements. Study sessions were programmed in the evening on weekdays. Outside Duntroon, cadets tended to go about in groups, and because of such distinguishing features as their short hair-cuts and relatively conservative civilian dress they were usually recognizable as Duntroon cadets. When they socialized in the wider community there were potential problems. Canberrans consistently vote for candidates who are to the left rather than to the right of the political spectrum, whereas cadets typically hold views and attitudes to the right of the political spectrum. Canberra is the site of the Australian National University, and in social contexts cadets inevitably came into contact with these university students of their own age group. While it is true that Australian university students in the 1980s were certainly more conservative than their predecessors in the 1960s and 1970s, Duntroon cadets in the early 1980s continued to regard students from civilian universities with some suspicion (and this was probably in part a hangover from the Vietnam War period). Cadets mixed with the wider community, but they saw themselves as separate from it, and in many ways superior to it.

The Royal Military College, in the early 1980s met many of the requirements which Goffman attributes to "total institutions."[2] By "total institutions" Goffman means organizations in which groups of people spend much of their lives working, sleeping, and playing within the one institutional boundary. For most of us such activities occur far more diffusely, that is to say, "in different places, with different co-participants, under different authorities, and without an over-all rational plan."[3] As examples of rigorous and narrowly confining total institutions Goffman offers mental hospitals, prisons, monasteries, concentration camps, ships, boarding schools, army barracks, and so on. While there are clearly differences among these groups, they do share some important features:

> First, all aspects of life are conducted in the same place and under the same single authority. Second, each phase of the member's daily activity is carried on in the immediate company of a large batch of others, all of whom are treated alike and required to do the same thing together. Third, all phases of the day's activities are tightly scheduled, with one activity leading at a prearranged time into the next, the whole sequence of activities being imposed from above by a system of explicit formal rulings and a body of officials. Finally, the various enforced activities are brought together into a single rational plan purportedly designed to fulfill the official aims of the institution.[4]

A common feature of such institutions is that by necessity

their institutional structures are sharply foregrounded. A corollary of this is that a specialized language necessarily accrues, a language which constructs the salient features of the institution *and* the tension which must inevitably exist between the elite within the bonding institution and the disparate and random people without.

At Duntroon, much of this specialized language is concerned with the internal structuring of the College, especially the "class system" which divides the Corps into First, Second, Third and Fourth Class cadets. The Fourth Class cadets are at the bottom of the system, and the way they are treated by seniors bears resemblance to the way "plebes" are treated at West Point.[5] Special languages, however, do not exist in a vacuum, and they always position themselves within a larger societal structure. Flexner points to the importance of slang in creating a sense of group solidarity (especially important to the military in general, and to a military college in particular), and how this in turn demands the creation of a large number of pejorative terms for outsiders, terms which he describes as "counter-words": "In uttering the counter we don't care what the person is; we are pledging our own group loyalty, affirming our identity, and expressing our satisfaction at being accepted."[6] In the case of Duntroon, all civilians are outsiders, and therefore "counter-words" must be created for them.[7] Perhaps surprisingly, however, the area of greatest lexical density for outsiders involves terms for women.

The concern with women is of course not surprising in itself. A group of some 450 seventeen to twenty-two year old males will inevitably be interested in women, and peer-group pressure will just as inevitably lead to a concern with sexual prowess. There is, moreover, the concern to establish heterosexual credentials. While it is true that the Duntroon pejorative terms for women, in general terms, are in keeping with slang patterns of the wider community, they are nevertheless especially intense. One thing which is interesting about the terms for women at Duntroon is how closely they are in keeping with the observations M.A.K. Halliday makes about what he calls antilanguages. It is common knowledge that "total institutions," which are highly specialized forms of secondary socialization, almost invariably develop their own special languages. At their extreme (as in prisons, or in a well-established criminal underworld) these total institutions are also anti-societies, and will develop anti-languages.

Halliday notes that in antilanguages the vocabulary is relexicalized (i.e., new words are created to replace some words in the primary language), and it is also overlexicalized (i.e., a number of denotatively synoymous but connotatively different words are created for a single item in the primary language; e.g. the plethora of terms in the Duntroon lexical system for "woman" or "girlfriend"). The vocabulary is overlexicalized first because within the sub-culture language is used for "verbal competition and display," and secondly because within the sub-culture social values are more clearly foregrounded than in the wider community.[8] Duntroon has certainly never been an "anti-society" in this extreme sense, and since the college is a military institution it could be argued that it is the embodiment or the preserver of the patriarchy's most conservative values. Nevertheless, just as the college shares many features of total institutions, so the lexical habits of its cadets share many features of anti-languages.

The Duntroon lexical system divides women into **bush mags** and **parade mags**. A **bush mag** is "an ugly or not so attractive girl(friend); a girl who is useful for a good night out but is not a contender for a serious relationship." The term derives from **bush magazine** (usually abbreviated to **bush mag**), the rifle magazine which a cadet uses when "out bush" on military training. This **bush mag** usually shows the effects of wear and tear ("really beaten up and a mess," as one respondent put it), and is contrasted with the well cared for and seemingly virginal magazine used on parade, the **parade mag** ("we have very immaculate rifle magazines for parades," as the same respondent put it). Thus a **parade mag** is "a girlfriend who, like the 'immaculate' magazine, is reserved for special functions; a 'nice,' 'respectable,' and indisputably 'good-looking' girl, especially one from 'home'; a good-looking girl suitable to be 'shown off' on occasions such as special parades; a 'serious' girlfriend—all these in contrast with the **bush mag**, the girl for 'everyday use'." In other terms, the basic contrast is between women who are available primarily for marriage and women who are available primarily for sex. Since cadets are not allowed to marry while at the college, variants of the term **parade mag** are not greatly needed, and there are very few variants for this concept. **Bush mag** and **parade mag** are examples of relexicalization. It is in extensions of the concept **bush mag** that overlexicalization occurs.

While this kind of division of women into the categories of "virgins" and "whores" is a commonplace of patriarchal societies, it is not usually foregrounded as blatantly and as insistently. All-male institutions such as college fraternities and some university colleges provide comparable social institutions, and often breed comparable attitudes. Yet such institutions differ markedly from Duntroon. The military environment excludes women as a matter of policy, and the Duntroon graduate belongs to an elite group in the officer ranks of the Australian army. Women could have no part in the institutional structure of Duntroon, and this in turn no doubt encouraged or intensified the patriarchal notion of the inferiority of women. Indeed, to give women any kind of status would obviously threaten the reality-sustaining strategies of the institution. At the same time women are seen as necessary evils. First, there is an official need for them—they are necessary adjuncts at social occasions such as mixed dining-in nights, and they are necessary social adjuncts as wives after graduation. Secondly, there is an unofficial need for them—a cadet's "manliness" must be proved sexually. These two needs are not necessarily in conflict, and indeed they may complement one another.

For example, take the term **tennis party**. At the end of the five-week induction period for Fourth Class cadets, this social function enables the new cadets to meet girls from the senior classes of the local secondary schools. It includes a dance in the evening. The *Cadet Handbook* (an official publication issued to all new cadets) gives the "authorized version":

> This function is organised for the benefit of Fourth Class, and is held in the First Term, normally on a Sunday. It is probably the first opportunity the new cadets have of meeting the young ladies of Canberra.

This function is organised for the benefit of Fourth Class, and is held This function is organised for the benefit of Fourth Class, and is held The encounter with "the young ladies of Canberra," however, is known by the cadets themselves as the **Fourth Class meat market**, the term **meat market** being slang for "a place where women are easily procurable for sex." In early 1983 there was an inquiry into alleged "hazing" of Fourth Class cadets by senior cadets, and there was much newspaper publicity about the charges. In *The Age* (Melbourne), 2 April 1983, a former cadet claimed that he received an "unofficial briefing" for the **tennis party** from a First Class cadet:

> He [the First Class cadet] had a list which went something like this: The meat market arrives at 1600 hours. At 1900 hours you will have them in the sportsman's bar. By 1930 hours you will have them drunk. By 2000 hours they should do anything you want them to. At Kokoda Company they had a points score system for each item of girls' underclothing brought back.

In the official version the **tennis party** is an important social ritual, as the cadets make social contact with the "young ladies" from Canberra's private schools; in the unofficial version it is a sexual game and ritual played out with military terminology and precision. The cadets' language constructs an image of **bush mag** women in terms of status and function. Because these are women for sex their status must be low, and the most common terms for them are **grogan** (common slang for the literal "turd") and **maggot**, and compounds thereof. Function is indicated by terms which indicate a view of women as masturbation-substitutes or masturbation receptacles: **blow rag, body to wank into, cum bucket, cum catcher, deluxe willie warmer, fuck bag, life support system for a cunt, night deposit for sperm, schlong holder, seminal spittoon, sperm bank, sperm bank on legs, sperm catcher, sperm receptacle, wanking machine.** Since, cadets aver, many women find **cordies** irresistible, terms must likewise be found for the **cordie-groupies**; thus terms such as **apple, bike, cordie maggot, corps root.**

Some of the terms which I have included in the list would not be regarded by cadets to be pejorative. These would include: **deluxe willie warmer, eleven, oui, parade mag, ten, weeee, willie warmer.** Even so, they are terms which encode attitudes which women would find utterly offensive.

Cadets have protested that many of these terms are not used seriously, and that they typically occur in boasting, teasing, or "flyting" inter-cadet conversations in the recreation rooms. But this of course precisely fits Halliday's argument that overlexicalization is caused partly by the need for a variety of terms in "verbal competition and display." Moreover, this is significantly a group phenomenon. Whether or not any individual cadet has these attitudes towards women is irrelevant. It is the system which, in constructing its own social reality and values, insists on the construction of this concept of women. While most of the terms within the non-Duntroon-specific areas of lexical density are known to all cadets, some are not. In these areas especially, one is dealing not simply with a mass of existing terms, but rather with a system which is capable of borrowing terms from the wider community or of generating its own terms. Many of the terms which I have included in the list are known in the wider community, although not many of them have found their way into slang dictionaries. In the Word List below, definitions (or parts of definitions) within quotation marks are usually cadet formulations.

WORD LIST

apple punning epithet for a woman with a reputation for promiscuous sexual activity with cadets—i.e., a woman who is "good to the Corps/core"

atrocity an extremely ugly woman. The term also appears in the phrase *to commit an atrocity*, which refers to the act of having sexual intercourse with an ugly woman. There is also a tradition among cadets that if a cadet is having sex with an ugly woman he must utter the term *atrocity* three times when coming to a sexual climax.

bag an unattractive woman. Common slang.

bag job an ugly woman, so called "because she needs a bag on her head to make her presentable." Sometimes intensified as a **two bag job**, **three bag job**, etc., according to the speaker's perception of the degree of ugliness involved.

bike a woman with a reputation for promiscuity among cadets, i.e., "everyone rides her"

Bin grogan a woman who is "good for a screw" but nothing else. The term *Bin* is a shortening of *The Private Bin*, a night club much frequented by cadets. It is assumed by cadets that women who visit the night club are on the lookout for sex, and are easy "scores." *See* GROGAN for the full connotations.

blow rag a woman (regarded as a masturbation substitute); a girlfriend; a woman with whom a cadet is having a sexual relationship. Although the term *blow rag* does not appear in dictionaries, it is a common term for a handkerchief (i.e., "a piece of rag into which one blows one's nose"). The cadet usage probably arises from the process (a) a handkerchief is something you may use to masturbate into ("blow" in the sense "ejaculate one's semen"), (b) a woman is an "object" to be ejaculated into.

body to wank into a woman; a girlfriend. The term *wank* is common slang for "masturbate," and the phrase therefore views the woman as a kind of "masturbation machine."

boff bag a woman. The term *boff* is a variant of *boof*, and both mean "fuck." Cf. FUCK BAG

boof bag a woman; a girlfriend. The term *boof* exists as a noun meaning "a fuck" and a verb meaning "to fuck," and therefore a *boof bag* is a woman whose only interest for a cadet is her availability for sex.

bush mag an ugly woman; a girl who is useful for a good night out, but is not a contender for a serious relationship. The term derives from *bush magazine* (usually abbreviated to *bush mag*), the rifle magazine which a cadet uses when "out bush" (i.e., out in the countryside) on military training. The *bush mag* usually shows the effects of wear and tear, and it is contrasted with the well cared for and seemingly virginal magazine used on parade, the *parade mag*. The connotations of the term *bush mag* when applied to a woman depend on the contrast between the *bush mag* and the *parade mag*.

bush pig a very ugly woman; an ugly army woman; a girlfriend — usually with the implication that this is a woman who is not especially socially or sexually desirable, but who will suffice for a brief sexual liaison. Sometimes abbreviated to *bushie*. The term is not in the dictionaries, but it appears in Kathy Lette's novel *Girls' Night Out* (Sydney, 1987), p. 187:

> Surfers are an amphibious, beach dwelling species, who hunt in packs for females with "margarine legs." You know, easily spread. Chicks are nicknamed bush pigs, swamp hogs, maggots, spitters or swallowers.

Its Australian usage is also noted in *Maledicta* 9 (1986–87), p. 93.

bushie *see* BUSH PIG

buzzard an ugly woman, with connotations of the predatory; an epithet reserved for the description of any other cadet's girlfriend (usually with the implication that she is not especially attractive and/or that she has "got her hooks" into him).

civie twat a civilian woman who is available for sex. The term *twat* is common slang for "vulva."

cordie girl a girl with a reputation for going out with and/or having sex with a large number of cadets. The term *cordie* means "a Duntroon cadet," and it is used by cadets themselves as well as by members of the wider community. It probably derives from a "Mandrake the Magician" cartoon which appeared in a popular Australian journal in the 1940s. The sinister Baron Kord used a magical powder to turn men into the "living dead" (called "Kordies"). He built up an army of these mindless servants with the aim of taking over the world. At first the term was used pejoratively of cadets by the wider community, but once its origin had been forgotten the pejorative connotations were lost.

cordie maggot a woman who is especially keen on cadets. *See* CORDIE GIRL and MAGGOT

corps root a woman who has sexual relations with many members of the Corps of Staff Cadets. *See* ROOT

corps whore a woman who tries to become part of the social scene at Duntroon, and is ever willing to offer sexual favours to members of the Corps of Officer Cadets in order to do so; a woman who transfers her sexual favours from cadet to cadet, and who appears to enjoy having sex with a lot of cadets.

cum bag a woman regarded exclusively as sexual object, i.e., as a bag to collect semen

cum bucket same as CUM BAG

cum catcher a woman regarded exclusively as sexual object, i.e., as a utensil to catch semen

cum kitten a sexually available woman. This term is no doubt a variation of *sex-kitten*.

cunt with body attached a woman; a girlfriend—or rather, all of a woman (or of a girlfriend) seen merely as an appendage or an accessory to the vital thing, the thing itself, the *sine qua non*, the *cunt*.

dead fuck a woman who in the act of sex is mechanical, cold, or otherwise unsatisfactory

exercise bike a woman; a girlfriend. *See* BIKE

deluxe willie warmer a woman with an especially satisfying vagina; a girlfriend. Here *willie* means "penis"; the term *willie warmer* perhaps derives from the sort of (jocular) "toys" illustrated in "adult" mail-order catalogues and provided by "adults-only" entrepreneurs for the stimulation of their "adults-only" customers, e.g., *willie warmer* (plain and deluxe)—a knitted cover for the penis, comparable to a knitted tea-cosy: hence a *deluxe* willie warmer.

denethor argabag a very ugly woman. Origin of term unknown. Cf. HERFERTIT ARGABAG

dick warmer a woman. Cf. DELUXE WILLIE WARMER

eleven (an) "a ten who swallows," i.e., an extremely attractive and sexually desirable woman (a ten-out-of-ten) who is willing to perform fellatio and swallow the semen, thereby achieving the rare distinction of being an eleven out of ten. *See* TEN

fid mag a rifle magazine, used when out in the field, which is usually in a somewhat battered condition as distinct from the PARADE MAG(AZINE) which is kept in immaculate condition for use on parade; by extension, an ugly woman, a girl who is useful for a good night out but is not a contender for a serious relationship. *See* the synonymous BUSH MAG. The *fid* element is the common cadet spelling of "FD," which is the official military abbreviation of "field."

fid woman variant of *fid mag* (q.v.)

flesh a woman; a girlfriend

fluff a woman; a girlfriend

front bum the external female genitalia; hence, by synecdoche, any female (especially a female soldier)

fuck bag a woman believed by cadets to be a "good fuck" and/or readily available for a fuck. Often with the implication: "She may be ugly, but she's willing to have sex with anyone."

fuck hole the vulva; hence, by synecdoche, a woman

fugly an unsightly woman; a term one cadet might use ribbingly of the girlfriend of another. A blending of *fucking* and *ugly.*

gash the female genitals; hence, by synecdoche, a woman; a girlfriend. Fairly common slang.

gash slut a promiscuous woman. Individually, the two terms of the compound are common slang.

grogan an ugly woman. This is one of the most intensely used terms, and it is sometimes abbreviated to **grogo** or **groge** (rhyming with "rogue"). In Australian slang *grogan* is a term for "turd," and this is no doubt the origin of the cadet usage.

hand-brake a girlfriend. The origin of this term is unclear. The most likely explanation is that the girlfriend is so called because she "puts the brake" on the cadet's otherwise "freewheeling" sexual joy-rides—and this was suggested by some respondents. One respondent, however, picked up the "hand" element of the metaphor: "she puts 'the brake' on a cadet's hand so he has no need (or opportunity) to masturbate."

herfertit argabag an ugly woman. Origin unclear. Cf. DENETHOR ARGABAG

horror bag an ugly woman

horror hag an ugly woman

horror head an ugly woman

horror show an ugly woman

horror smash an ugly woman

life support system for a cunt a woman—or rather all of a woman with the exception of her cunt: the only reason for the woman's existence is to keep the cunt functional. Synonym: **life support system for a vagina**

lowie an "easy" or promiscuous woman. In general Australian slang this has appeared as a form of "low-heel," i.e., a sexually promiscuous woman; but the Duntroon usage may be an independent formulation, indicating one who is "low" on the "moral scale."

mag a woman; a girlfriend. Probably an abbreviation of MAGGOT (q.v.), but perhaps an abbreviation of BUSH MAG (q.v.)

maggot a woman; a girlfriend. A woman so described is usually regarded as being a very temporary sexual partner, on the grounds of appearance or of social status. The term *maggoting* is used to describe the activity of "going out looking for a woman"; if the quest is successful the claim "I scored a *maggot*" is likely to be heard. The connotations of the Duntroon *maggot* probably derive from the literal grub or worm. The term appears occasionally in Australian slang in the sense "a despicable, despised person," but the Duntroon term is applied exclusively to women, and its use is especially intense.

mattress a woman; a girlfriend—a woman who is always on her back and ready for sex. The woman serves as a mattress, i.e., one lies on her. Cf. German soldiers' slang *Armeematratze* "army mattress" and *Offiziersmatratze* "officer's mattress," a promiscuous woman who has sex with officers and soldiers; a whore. [9]

mattress-back a promiscuous woman. Cf. MATTRESS

meat flesh, i.e., a female body as sexual object. Common slang.

mess maggot a female member of the catering staff in the Mess of the Corps of Officer Cadets; a woman so called usually has a reputation for socializing with cadets, and being available for sex.

mess pig Synonymous with MESS MAGGOT

mole a woman with a reputation for promiscuity; someone else's girlfriend. Common slang.

muck hole the vagina (bowdlerized form of "fuck hole") and, by extension, a woman

night deposit for sperm a woman, especially one viewed as befitting a fuck and nothing else. The term appears to have arisen by analogy with a bank's "night deposit" box, i.e., a slotted receptacle into which customers deposit cash "after hours"; hence a woman is a slotted receptacle into which cadets may deposit their sperm "after hours."

oui French for "yes," used to designate an attractive "yes woman," i.e., a woman who readily agrees to sexual demands of various kinds.

parade mag a girlfriend who is reserved for special functions; a "nice," "respectable," and indisputably "good-looking" girl, especially one from "home"; a good-looking girl suitable to be "shown off" on occasions such as special parades and other important social functions; a "serious" girlfriend—all these in contrast with the BUSH MAG (q.v.)

parade woman a good-looking woman. Synonymous with PARADE MAG

piece of flesh a woman, especially a woman seen as sexual object

pig a woman, especially one perceived to be particularly ugly. Cf. BUSH PIG

pillow biter a woman in the context of especially aggressive or passionate sexual intercourse, when the male exclaims: "Bite the pillow, bitch!" The phrase "to bite the pillow" here means "to suppress a scream of delight" caused by being fucked well. Such terminology is used mainly in boasting recreation room conversation. Also applied to a woman who "does a doggy," that is, who goes on all fours and allows the male to enter from behind (not, however, anally). It is this canine proclivity that is usually referred to in the stock cadet questions: "Did you make her bite the pillow?" and "Is she a pillow biter?" Cf. SQUEAL MACHINE

piss-flaps on legs a woman. From *piss-flaps* in the slang sense "the labia; vulva."

pork a woman, as sexual object. The term *pork* is also used in the more common slang sense of "penis," but the sense "woman" derives from *pork* = "female flesh," i.e., the vulva, hence, by synecdoche, a woman seen simply as a sexual object.

RBT a woman; a girlfriend. *R.B.T.* is the common Australian initialism of "Road Breathalyser Test" or "Random Breath Test" wherein a person suspected of driving a car when he has an alcohol level above the legal limit is required to blow into a bag for the testing of his alcohol level; the punning involved in the usage-transference here is along these lines: "You have to be drunk to blow" ("blow" in the sense "to ejaculate") into a *bag* (q.v.), or

"You have to be drunk to blow" (i.e., to perform cunnilingus on) a *bag*. Thus, among the definitions supplied by respondents, are: "A bag (with allusion to *bag* in the sense "an ugly woman") you blow when you're pissed" (i.e., drunk); and (less commonly) "You've got to be pissed (drunk) to blow into them."

root a fuck; also a woman (in the sense "rootee") as in "she's a good *root*." The term *root* is common Australian slang for "penis" (from its fancied resemblance to the underground part of a plant, e.g., a carrot); hence the verb *to root* = to fuck.

root bag a woman; a girlfriend. Variant of the more common term FUCK BAG (q.v.)

root rat a woman with a reputation for sexual promiscuity

schlong holder a woman; a girlfriend. The *schlong* element is common slang for "penis," which in turn derives from the Yiddish for "snake." The term *holder* here is vaginal, not manual: just as a scabbard is a "sword holder," so the woman (via vagina) is a s*chlong holder.*

scrag a woman, especially one who is ugly, sleazy, tartish, of no more worth to the viewing male than as a NIGHT DEPOSIT FOR SPERM (q.v.). Synonymous with GROGAN (q.v.). Appears in common slang as a verb meaning "to have sexual intercourse."

scrubber a woman with a reputation for being "rough," "loose," "easy." Common slang for a promiscuous but unattractive woman.

scruff a woman. Used especially in the phrases "a bit of scruff," "a piece of scruff."

semen receptacle a girlfriend; sexual partner; woman. Cf. NIGHT DEPOSIT FOR SPERM, SPERM RECEPTACLE, etc.

seminal spittoon same as SEMEN RECEPTACLE

slag a girlfriend; a disgusting woman. Common slang for a promiscuous woman.

slag bag a repulsively ugly woman; also (in inter-cadet conversation) a girlfriend

slag heap a "dilapidated" woman, an ugly mess of a woman; also (in inter-cadet conversation) a girlfriend

slime bag a (usually) disreputable woman, a woman of low moral standing

slut a girlfriend—usually one whom a cadet sees for sex only, and in whom he has no further interest whatsoever, or one who accompanies a cadet on a social outing, but in whom he has no real interest. Common slang for a promiscuous woman.

sperm bank a girlfriend, a woman. Also in the term *sperm bank on legs*. Clearly a transfer from the technical term, the repository for storing sperm for use in artificial insemination.

sperm catcher a girlfriend, a woman. Cf. CUM CATCHER

sperm receptacle a girlfriend, a woman. Cf. SEMINAL SPITTOON

split arse a girlfriend, a woman. The term *split-arsed one* is sometimes used in general slang for a female.

squeal machine a girlfriend; a female sexual machine. Alludes to the noises of delight emitted by the woman in response to the supposed superlative sexual prowess of the cadet. Cf. PILLOW BITER

tag rag a girlfriend. The term *tag* is Duntroon specific slang for "masturbation," and a *tag rag* is a towel or other piece of cloth used for wiping up the results of masturbation. The Duntroon usage "girlfriend" most likely derives from the process (a) a *tag rag* is something you ejaculate into when you masturbate; (b) a girlfriend is someone you ejaculate into; therefore (c) a girlfriend is a *tag rag*. Cf. BLOW RAG

tart a woman, especially one with a reputation for promiscuity, "an easy lay." Common slang.

ten a highly attractive and desirable woman (i.e., a ten-out-of-ten, thus a woman who is a nonpareil, a *ne plus ultra*). Probably influenced by the film *10* by Blake Edwards. Cf. ELEVEN

ten bag job an inordinately ugly woman, the antithesis of a TEN (q.v.). *See* BAG JOB for further details.

ten that swallows (a) *see* ELEVEN

Terry Dactyl a girlfriend; an ugly woman. A corruption of *pterodactyl*.

the fuck a woman with whom a cadet is having a sexual relationship. Note the use of the definite article.

three bag job *see* BAG JOB

thumb print a girlfriend. A cadet who is regarded as being "under the thumb" of his girlfriend is often accused of having a bald patch the size of a thumb on his head; by extension, the girlfriend is often referred to as the *thumb print*.

tunnel the vagina; hence, by synecdoche, a woman (seen entirely in terms of "her only useful part")

two bag job *see* BAG JOB

vac flaps a woman perceived as being (or believed to be) sexually high-powered and possessed of an insatiable vulva (the *vac flaps* in question): i.e., she is "a woman who is a good fucker," "a girl with sexual desires like a vacuum cleaner." The term derives from *flaps* understood as "lips," in this instance the *labia majora* and *minora*, + *vac*, back-clipping of *vacuum* (as in *vacuum cleaner*), hence "powerful suctorial."

wanking machine a girlfriend, a woman. From *wank* in the sense "to masturbate."

weeee a girlfriend; a good-looking woman. Perhaps a variant of OUI (q.v.)

wench a girlfriend, often in the form *the wench*. Common slang, but distinctive in the form with the definite article as a term for one's girlfriend.

the whore a temporary girlfriend; a woman who is useful for sex

willie warmer a woman, seen as provider of sexual comfort to the male (*willie* being common slang for "penis"). See DELUXE WILLIE WARMER

wizzer a woman. Also in the form **wizzie**. The term *wizzer* is used for both the penis and the vagina.

wizzie same as **wizzie**

woman a girlfriend. Often with possessive adjectives or the definite article: *my woman*, *the woman*, *your woman*.

FOOTNOTES

[1] Some terms from the early 1950s appear in Sidney Baker's *Australia Speaks* (Sydney: Shakespeare Head Press, 1953). Eric Partridge's *A Dictionary of Slang*, 8th edition, ed. Paul Beale (London: Routledge & Kegan Paul, 1984) includes **(the) clink** as a Duntroon term for the College itself, **mash** in the sense "to study very hard," and **stook** in the sense "a cigarette."

[2] Erving Goffman, *Asylums* (New York: Doubleday, 1961).

[3] *Asylums*, pp. 6–7.

[4] *Asylums*, p. 6.

[5] Sanford M. Dornbusch, "The Military Academy as an Assimilating Institution," *Social Forces* 33 (1955), pp. 316–21, describes a similar system at the United States Coast Guard Academy.

[6] *Dictionary of American Slang*, ed. Harold Wentworth and Stuart Berg Flexner, 2nd supplemented ed. (New York: Thomas Crowell, 1975), p. xi.

[7] There are abusive terms for groups such as public servants, homosexuals, and so on; apart from women, the major recipients of abusive epithets, however, are people of non-Anglo-Saxon origin, especially Asians.

[8] M.A.K. Halliday, "Antilanguages," in his *Language as Social Semiotic: The Social Interpretation of Language and Meaning* (London: Edward Arnold, 1978), pp. 164–82.

[9] I am grateful to Dr. Aman for the analogies in German slang.

CHEMICAL ANALYSIS OF WOMAN

Element: Woman
Symbol: ♀
Discoverer: Adam
Atomic Mass: Officially accepted as 53.4 kg, but know to vary from 40 to 225 kg
Occurrence: Copious quantities throughout the world

Physical Properties
1. Surface usually covered with film of powder and paint
2. Boils at absolutely nothing and freezes for no apparent reason
3. Melts if given special treatment
4. Bitter if incorrectly used
5. Found in various states from virgin material to common ore
6. Yields to pressure when applied at correct points

Chemical Properties
1. Has great affinity to gold, silver, platinum, and precious stones
2. Absorbs great quantities of expensive substances
3. Explodes spontaneously for no known reason
4. Insoluble in liquids, but activity greatly increases when saturated with alcohol
5. The most powerful money-reducing agent known to man

Common Uses
1. Highly decorative, especially in sports cars
2. Can greatly aid relaxation
3. Can be a very effective cleaning agent

Tests
1. Pure specimens turn rosy pink when discovered in natural state
2. Turns green when placed alongside a superior specimen

Hazards
1. Highly explosive in inexperienced hands
2. Possession of more than one is illegal, although several can be maintained at different locations provided specimens do not come in direct contact with each other
WARNING: Prolonged exposure to this element can cause severe physical, mental, and financial damage!

Thanks to David Broome & Stephen Silver

DYSPHEMISM AND EUPHEMISM IN THE EROTICA OF HENRY MILLER AND ANAÏS NIN

Joe Darwin Palmer

In 1941 and 1942 Henry Miller wrote erotic stories for Milton Luboviski, a bookseller, according to an affidavit that Luboviski filed at the American Embassy in Paris on March 10, 1983. Luboviski's memory was probaby a little short, for, according to *The Diary of Anaïs Nin* in April 1940, Miller started writing erotica for money. In December 1940, Nin started writing erotic stories for the same client. The writers were paid at the rate of one dollar per page.

The stories were later collected and published commercially, Miller's with the title *Opus Pistorum* in 1983 by Grove Press. This title was changed to *Under the Roofs of Paris* in 1985. Some of Nin's stories were published with the title *Delta of Venus* by Harcourt in 1977. Others with the title *Little Birds* appeared in 1979.

The word choice in these stories illustrates differences between men's and women's language, in spite of Harriet Zinnes' assertion in *The New York Times Book Review*, n.d., that Nin's stories "are...the first American stories by a woman to celebrate sexuality with complete and open abandonment." Even though Nin tried to "leave out the poetry," as demanded by her client, she was "conscious of a difference between the masculine and feminine treatment of sexual experience," and "knew that there was a great disparity between Henry Miller's explicitness and [her] ambiguities—between his humorous, Rabelaisian view of sex and [her] poetic descriptions...(*Delta of Venus*, xiv)."

The first story in *Under the Roofs of Paris* is entitled "Sous les Toits de Paris." The first story in *Delta of Venus* is "The Hungarian Adventurer." Each is about 2300 words in length.

The terms in these stories relating to sexual organs and body parts, and to copulation are grouped under three rubrics (numbers indicate occurrences):

MALE GENITALS, ETC.

Miller		**Nin**	
balls	2	hair	I
bush	3	penis	II
cock	10		
dick	4		
dong	II		
Jean Jeudi	I		
John Thursday	4		
jism	2		
prick	2		

FEMALE GENITALS, ETC.

Miller		**Nin**	
ass	4	bodies	I
bodies	I	body	I
breasts	I	breasts	4
bubs	I	bud	I
bush	3	sex	3
cunt	5	thighs	I
cuntlet	4		
figlet	I		
gates	I		
hairy nest	I		
hole	I	**Miller** (continued)	
hot pocket	I	meat	I
itch under her tail	I	mousetrap	2
legs	I	nipples	2

Miller (continued)

ripe fig	1
split fig	1
stable	1
tail	1
teats	1

Miller (continued)

thighs	1
trap	1
whiskers	2
womb	5
wound	1

COPULATION, ETC.

Miller

come	3
diddle	11
fuck	18
have laid	1
screw	1
suck	4
suck off	1

Nin

caress	2
catch	1
come	1
feel through their nightgowns	1
fondle	2
force himself on	1
grasp	1
hand grip	1
hand went everywhere	1
incest	1
kiss	5
kneading	1
make love to	1
possess	1
reach his pleasure	1
rubbing	1
sit astride	1
slipped his hands along	1
sucked	1
teasing	2

We can see in the above lists that Miller emphasizes the body, while Nin emphasizes making love. Additionally, we see that Miller uses 114 of such terms, while Nin uses only 50. Miller's comic scatology breaks the verbal taboos of their day, just as Nin's euphemisms respect them.

QUEER SISTERS

Reinhold Aman

The Sisters of Perpetual Indulgence, a San Francisco group of male homosexuals who dress like Catholic nuns and enjoy "parodical and salacious names," have made it "a sort of parlor game" to coin new Sister names for themselves. Below are some of the best, from a longer list published in their newsletter, *The Nun Issue* I.2 (July 1993), p. 7.

Sister Baby Jane Bitch Lips
Sister Cum Lately?
Sister Flatulina Grande
Sister Florence Nightmare, R.N.
Sister Gladass of the Joyous
  Resurrectum
Sister Hellina Handbasket
Sister Homocycle Motorsexual
Sister Ivanna Tramp
Sister Jackie O'Nasty
Sister Latex of the Immaculate
  Protection
Sister Lily White Superior
  Posterior
Sister Lucretia Merciful Release
Sister Maria Maria Gonorrhea
Sister Nocturnal Omissions

Sister Okla Homo Sexual
Sister Opiate of the Masses
Sister Penis Fly Trap
Sister Phatima La Dyke Van Dick
Sister Queer As Can Be
Sister Sadie Sadie the Rabbi Lady
Sister Sleaze Du Jour
Sister Succuba
Sister Sybil War
Sister Teresa Stigmata
Sister There's No Place Like Rome
Sister Vaginita Dentata La
  Bufadora
Sister Vicious Power Hungry Bitch
Sister WHO the Hell Does He
  Think She Is?
Reverend Mother Suxcox

Thanks to Tom Slone

"JEW MOTHERFUCKER" AND "NIGGER"
The Foulmouthed & Lying Clintons

Reinhold Aman

Millions of cretinous and amoral Americans still admire Bill and Hillary Clinton, the two foulest amoral slimebags that have ever besmirched the White House. These two foulmouthed and lying psychopaths have been, and still are, blindly supported by masses of non-clinical morons, diehard Democrats, and whorish liberal journalists and their editors.

Lest you think I am a Republican, conservative, or member of the imaginary "vast right-wing conspiracy": I am an apolitical anti-politician. Because I despise blatantly lying politicians with all my guts, I am presenting this uncensored record of some of the foul language used by these two parasitical pieces of putrid puke that have lived off the taxpayers of Arkansas and the United States for many years—thanks to partisan, knee-jerk or imbecilic supporters. Anyone who admires or supports those two amoral swine is just as amoral as they are.

The Foulmouthed First Bitch & Senator
The following five quotations are from Alec Flegon's *Dictionary of English Sex Quotations* (London: Flegon Press, 1996):

▶ L.D. Brown, a member of Clinton's former security staff and bodyguard in Arkansas, stated that Hillary is "**as foulmouthed as any sailor you'd ever meet.**" (p. 147)
▶ As reported by Bill's security staff, Hillary **frequently erupted in expletive-filled tirades** against him. "I can't believe you would ask a **fucking** question like that!" Or, about his shaky driving, "You're gonna get us **fucking** killed!" (p. 147)
▶ She shouted at Bill over his unfaithfulness: "**I need to be fucked** more than twice a year!" (p. 170)

▶ Hillary to Larry Patterson, an Arkansas state trooper and Clinton bodyguard from 1986 to 1993, who was bringing a judge's wife to the Little Rock airport: "What the **fuck** do you think you're doing? I know who that **whore** is." (p. 171)

▶ Coming out of the Arkansas governor's mansion early morning on Labor Day 1991, Hillary screamed: "Where is the **goddamn fucking** flag? I want the **goddamn fucking** flag up every **fucking** morning at **fucking** sunrise!" (p. 173).

～

Patterson observed Hillary standing at the bottom of the stairs in the governor's mansion, and Bill at the top of the stairs with little Chelsea beside him, as Hillary screamed at him at the top of her lungs: "**Goddamn stupid fucking fool!**" [NewsMax, 15 July 2000]

Patterson stated that Bill and Hillary Clinton would frequently argue with each other **using the worst expletives known to mankind**, sometimes in the presence of their daughter Chelsea. Some of the anti-Semitic slurs with which she commonly laced her tirades against Bill were "**Jew motherfucker**," "**Jew Boy**" and "**Jew Bastard.**" [NewsMax, 15 and 17 July 2000]

"If she disagreed with Bill Clinton or she disagreed with some of the Jewish community in Little Rock—or some of the ethnic community—she would often make these statements." "She would say '**Jew Bastard**' or call her husband a '**Jew boy**' or a '**motherfucking Jew**'," Patterson told the WABC New York radio audience. [Carl Limbacher and NewsMax Staff, 17 July 2000]

Patterson said he heard Hillary "utter **anti-Jewish epithets** between 10 and 20 times over the course of his six years at the Arkansas governor's mansion." [NewsMax, 17 July 2000]

Hillary's rages continued after she took up residence in the White House, where she blew up at a Secret Service agent for declining to carry her bags. When the agent explained that he needed to keep his hands free in order to protect her, she replied: "If you want to remain on this detail, get your **fucking ass** over here and grab those bags." [Joyce Milton in *The First Partner: Hillary Rodham Clinton* (1999), p. 259]

Hillary to a Secret Service agent, after she heard that a University of California–Berkeley student had written a satirical column in *The Daily Californian* about daughter Chelsea: "What the **fuck** is going on?" [*San Francisco Chronicle*, 26 Nov. 1997]

Bill also badmouthed others and his dear Hillary. David Brock, ex-*American Spectator* reporter: "From the back of his Lincoln, Bill Clinton would say about Paula Jones, 'What does that **whore** think she's doing to me?' He also referred to his ex-lover Gennifer Flowers as a '**fucking slut**,' according to Larry Patterson." [Drudge Report, 9 March 1998]

When Hillary (once again) physically attacked Bill, Secret Service agents had to separate them. "Keep that **bitch** away from me!" Bill Clinton told one Secret Service agent. [*The National Enquirer*, 5 Jan. 1999]

"Nigger"

Larry Patterson confirmed that he frequently heard Bill Clinton use "**nigger**" to refer to both Jesse Jackson and local Little Rock black leader Robert "Say" McIntosh. Longtime Clinton paramour Dolly Kyle Browning corroborated Patterson on Clinton's use of "**nigger**." "Not only did he use the '**N' word**, he called him a '**GDN**' [**goddamn nigger**], if you catch my drift," Browning told Fox News in 1999. [NewsMax, 17 July 2000]

Brown also told NewsMax that the president would regularly make **derogatory comments about African-Americans** in private. "He has used the '**N' word** before. Bill would make **snide remarks about blacks** behind their backs." [Carl Limbacher and NewsMax Staff, 17 July 2000]

Patterson said Hillary was no stranger to the "**N**" **word** either. He heard her say "**nigger**" "probably six, eight, ten times. She would be upset with someone in the black community and she would use the '**N' word**, like, you heard they've got the president's brother on tape using the '**N' word**." [NewsMax, 17 July 2000]

It's all in the family: Captured on videotape when Arkansas

state police had Hillary's brother-in-law Roger Clinton under surveillance for dealing cocaine in 1984, Roger stated: "Some junior high **nigger** kicked Steve's ass while he was trying to help his brothers out; junior high or sophomore in high school. Whatever it was, Steve had the **nigger** down. However it was, it was Steve's fault. He had the **nigger** down, he let him up. The **nigger** blindsided him." [NewsMax, 17 July 2000]

"You Fucking Jew Bastard!"

Jerry Oppenheimer's book *State of the Union: Inside the Complex Marriage of Bill and Hillary Clinton* (2000) quotes former campaign aide Mary Lee Fray, who says that Hillary exploded in a rage after Bill lost his first bid for elective office, a run for Congress in Arkansas's Third Congressional District against John Paul Hammerschmidt. Hillary blamed Fray's husband, Paul, for the campaign's bungled political strategy. The slur was uttered at a heated, finger-pointing session at Bill Clinton's Fayetteville, Ark., campaign headquarters on election night in 1974, following his defeat. "**You fucking Jew bastard!**" Hillary yelled at Paul, Mary Lee confirmed—even though Paul Fray is not Jewish. [NewsMax, 15 July 2000]

In the room that night were Bill Clinton; his then-girlfriend Hillary Rodham; Paul Fray, Clinton's campaign manager; and Fray's wife, Mary Lee. Another campaign worker, Neill McDonald, was just outside the door and heard everything. [*Daily News*, 17 July 2000] Paul Fray is a Baptist but his heritage is Jewish; his paternal grandmother was Jewish, and Bill and Hillary knew of his heritage.

Mary Lee Fray said that Hillary not only used **an anti-Semitic slur** but she shouted it so loudly "it rattled the walls." "It was very clear," she said. "Bill Clinton's face became white as a ghost." [FOXNews.com, AP and *New York Post*, 18 July 2000]

Former Clinton campaign aide Neill McDonald, who has always been a Clinton supporter [*Jewish World Review*, 19 July 2000], confirmed the story, according to the New York *Daily News*. [Reuters, 17 July 2000] He heard the obscenity as he stood outside the room. [FOXNews.com, AP, *New York Post*, 18 July 2000]

The Usual Media Coverup

Sources in Arkansas told mainstream reporters as early as 1999 about Hillary Clinton's use of **anti-Semitic language**, but they and their editors decided to withhold the bombshell revelation from the American people. [NewsMax, 18 July 2000]

Vanity Fair writer Gail Sheehy, who has enjoyed special access to Mrs. Clinton over the years, interviewed Mary Lee Fray for her book *Hillary's Choice*. Sheehy told *Newsday* that even though Mary Lee's account included Mrs. Clinton's vile slur, her husband made no mention of it in a separate interview. Sheehy does not say that Mr. Fray denied the story—only that the subject did not come up. Apparently the author herself decided to avoid the topic, thereby ruling out any chance that a second source for Hillary's anti-Semitic shocker would compel publication. [NewsMax, 18 July 2000]

Sheehy said that she had heard the story of the alleged **anti-Semitic comment** several years ago from Fray's wife. But Sheehy said she left it out of her book because it was "off the wall. It was totally without credibility." [NewsMax, 18 July 2000]

NBC-TV's Andrea Mitchell admitted that Fray recounted the incident, complete with Hillary's **anti-Semitic slur**, during an interview for the network's "Dateline NBC" program in 1999. But NBC News editors decided to kill the report on the sensational allegation because the story lacked corroboration, Mitchell said. [NewsMax, 18 July 2000]

The folks at NBC must not have tried too hard to substantiate Fray's account, since his wife, Mary Lee, was more than willing to corroborate the charge—as she has for dozens of reporters since the story resurfaced. [NewsMax, 18 July 2000]

One-time Clinton consultant Dick Morris gave Gail Sheehy an exclusive account of his now legendary story about Hillary's use of a Jewish stereotype during an argument she had with him. "**Money—that's all you people care about is**

money," Morris said Hillary yelled after he asked for a pay raise in 1986. In November 1999 Morris went public with the story, noting that he'd told it to Sheehy for her then-upcoming Hillary biography, *Hillary's Choice.* But when the book hit the stands in December, Morris's explosive report was nowhere to be found. [NewsMax, 18 July 2000]

Hillary's Lying & Denying

Hillary called a news conference on her Chappaqua front lawn and angrily and tearfully said, "I wanted to unequivocally state **it never happened**, I hate this type of politics of destruction." [UPI, 17 July 2000]

Senate candidate Hillary Rodham Clinton **angrily denied** having uttered an anti-Jewish slur 26 years ago. "**I've never said anything like that in my entire life**," the first lady said. [Reuters, 16 July 2000]

Mrs. Clinton angrily denied making the ethnic slur, saying the report was "**absolutely false.**" [FOXNews.com, AP and *New York Post*, 18 July 2000]

Angry and emotional, Hillary Rodham Clinton **firmly denied** allegations from a forthcoming book that she used an anti-Semitic slur 26 years ago. [AP, 16 July 2000]

"I can only state unequivocally **it did not happen**," she said. "Any reasonable person looking at the evidence in this case would conclude **there's no credibility on the other side**." [Reuters, 17 July 2000]

Hillary: "I want to state unequivocally that **it never happened and very clearly point out that it goes against my entire life**," she said. "In the past, I may have called someone a name, but **I have never used ethnic, racial, anti-Semitic, bigoted, discriminatory, prejudiced accusations against anybody. I've never done it. I've never thought it.** So why people are accusing me of this is certainly beyond my understanding." [*Daily News*, 17 July 2000]

"I have a lot of confidence in the fundamental good judgment of New Yorkers to see through these kinds of charges," Mrs. Clinton said during a press conference on Ellis Island. [AP, 18 July 2000]

In addition to the above-cited anti-Semitic and anti-Black slurs by Hillary (and Bill), she used an anti-Italian slur against then-Senate candidate Al D'Amato in 1998 by publicly ridiculing him as '**Senator Tomato**'." [NewsMax, 17 July 2000]

Being a pathological liar, Hillary denies & denies & denies. It's sad and depressing that millions of moronic Americans believe her and that amoral, stupid or opportunistic New Yorkers elected that carpet-bagging bitch as a senator. It is to puke.

Bill's Denials, Lies & Contradictions

Is there anyone who does not remember the two most widely reported blatant lies by that psychopathic liar Bill Clinton? You know, that he "didn't inhale" when smoking marijuana and that he "did not have sexual relations with that woman, Miss Lewinsky." (I guess pot wasn't strong enough for "Cocaine Bill," whose half-brother Roger was caught on a police surveillance video saying, "Got to get some for my brother. He's got a nose like a vacuum cleaner." [*The Electronic Telegraph* (London), 15 July 1996])

The Clinton campaign released a statement from President Clinton in which he said: "I was there on election night in 1974 and **this charge is simply not true. It did not happen.** My wife has stood for social justice and tolerance and against racial and religious hatred and bigotry for as long as I have known her." [AP, 16 July 2000]

Clinton jumped to his wife's defense: "**She might have called him a bastard**," the president said in an interview in the New York *Daily News*. "I wouldn't rule that out. **She's never claimed that she was pure on profanity. But I've never heard her tell a joke with an ethnic connotation. She's so fanatic about it. She can't tell an ethnic joke—it's not in her.**" [UPI, 17 July 2000; *Daily News*, 17 July 2000; FOXNews, AP, and *New York Post*, 18 July 2000]

President Clinton came to his wife's defense, **denying that she called a campaign aide a "fucking Jew bastard"** in 1974. In two telephone calls to the New York *Daily News* from the Camp David Middle East summit, including one to

Mortimer B. Zuckerman, the paper's chairman and co-publisher, the President said, "**I was there and** [Hillary] **never said it. In 29 years, my wife has never, ever uttered an ethnic or racial slur against anybody, ever. She's so straight on this, she squeaks.**" [*Daily News*, 17 July 2000]

So Bill remembered the event but the lying bitch didn't? One wonders whether that foul female squeaked whenever she uttered "**nigger**," "**Jew motherfucker**," "**Jew boy**," and "**You fucking Jew bastard!**"

"It really got bad," Clinton said, "and he [Paul Fray] and Hillary somehow got in a fight. **There was never a racial slur.** If she were an anti-Semite, which she is not, it would never have occurred to her to say anything like that to him"—a reference to the fact that Fray is not Jewish. [*Daily News*, 17 July 2000]

Hillary's hubby exposed that lying cunt in a rare moment of telling the truth: He acknowledged that there was a fight, that she called Fray a "bastard," and implied that she used "fucking" ("She's never claimed that she was pure on profanity"), but then switched back to his standard *modus operandi* by lying that she didn't use "Jew." Why? Because that would have cost her the pivotal Jewish vote.

Others On the Clinton Denials

"I think they've got a little bit of what you call '**selective memory**'," Paul Fray added, referring to the president and first lady, who have vehemently denied the accusation. [FOXNews.com, AP and *New York Post*, 18 July 2000]

"I'm inclined to believe she did it. It's not because she has a vicious streak in her [and] has a notoriously bad temper; it's not because [Jewish] Dick Morris made a similar charge concerning a comment Hillary made to him when they were discussing his consulting fees: 'That's all you people care about is money.' **Hillary is telling the patently unbelievable story that she doesn't even remember the altercation with Fray, when even husband Bill admits remembering the fight.**" [David Limbaugh in *Jewish World Review*, 19 July 2000]

Defended By Sycophantic Double-Standard Jews
Various big-name Jews, such as the shameless Clinton-ass-sucking Senator Charles Schumer (N.Y.), former New York City Mayor Ed Koch, and Abe Foxman, head of the Anti-Defamation League, immediately came to Hillary's defense by claiming that she is not anti-Semitic— **despite her frequent anti-Semitic utterances, the Rodham family's well-known dislike of Jews, the Clintons' anti-Semitic jokes, and her repeated use of "Jew bastard" and "Jew motherfucker."**

"I don't believe she said it, and if she said it 26 years ago, so what?" Ed Koch, who makes no secret of being a proud Jew, told the *New York Post*. "Did she say it yesterday? There must be a statute of limitations." [NewsMax, 15 July 2000]

Abe Foxman told the *New York Post*, "If in fact she said it, that does not make her an anti-Semite, because there is a public record of Hillary Rodham Clinton of the past 26 years which has no iota of anti-Semitism." [NewsMax, 15 July 2000]

The ADL said in a statement that it believes the First Lady when she said she never called Paul Fray a "fucking Jew bastard" during an argument after the loss 26 years ago. [UPI, 17 July 2000]

Sen. Charles Schumer, who is Jewish, issued a statement saying, "I've known Hillary Clinton for eight years, and she doesn't have an anti-Semitic bone in her body." [Reuters, 16 July 2000]

Jewish New York Congresswoman Nita M. Lowey also defended Hillary: "...there's no way Hillary could make a statement like that." [AP, 16 July 2000]

Not All New York Jews Were That Shameless
Leaders of New York's Jewish community lined up on opposite sides of the debate. Representatives of conservative Jewish groups disagreed with the Anti-Defamation League's defense of Hillary. Dov Hikind, a New York Assemblyman and leader of Brooklyn's Orthodox Jewish community, told UPI: "If this was only a remark made 26 years ago, then it wouldn't be a big issue.... [But this] is not an isolated case." "There is no

statute of limitations for racism or anti-Semitism or bigotry."
[AP and Reuters, 17 July 2000]

Excerpts from Rabbi Dr. Morton H. Pomerantz, state chaplain for the State of New York: "Madame Hillary called a campaign aide a 'Fucking Jew Bastard.' Funny, isn't it, that Manhattan's limousine liberal Jewish set wants so quickly to forget about Hillary's anti-Semitism…. The liberal New York media —dominated as it is by members of the Jewish community— have barely mentioned the trooper's [Larry Patterson] allegations and has afforded Hillary every benefit of the doubt. Surely, if Mr. Lazio, her Senate opponent, had made such remarks about Jews—no matter how long ago—he would have been skewered by New York's liberal press like there was no tomorrow. **The major media have become inveterate ass-kissers of the Clintons….**" [NewsMax, 24 July 2000]

Media Censors & Weasels

There's no doubt that Hillary called Paul Fray a "fucking Jew bastard." If there were the slightest doubt, you can bet that vicious Hillary would have sicced her amoral $450-an-hour shyster David Kendall on every author, publication and news service that reported her anti-Semitic slur, regardless of how veiled and coy the media were about her vile outburst.

Following below is a sampling of how the media reported "fucking Jew bastard." Note the euphemized *fucking* and its suppression, the euphemized *bastard*, as well as the various uninformative paraphrases, verbal maneuvers, and spineless weaseling. The quotations are arranged from the most to the least complete reporting of Hillary's exact and complete filth. *Time* magazine wins the Weasel Prize for keeping the reader in the dark about what was actually said; the Associated Press is runner-up for euphemizing *bastard* and suppressing *fucking*; and United Press International wins third place for euphemizing all words but "Jew." A special prize goes to CBS Radio News for telling its listeners that Hillary merely "used rough language" and an unspecified "anti-Semitic slur"—like what? *Kike? Hebe? Christ-killer?*

Hillary's actual words: **"You fucking Jew bastard!"** [Jerry Oppenheimer in his book *State of the Union: Inside the Complex Marriage of Bill and Hillary Clinton* (2000)]

"f***ing Jew bastard" [*The Times* (London), 18 July 2000]
"f-----g Jew bastard" [New York *Daily News*, 17 July 2000]
"f****** Jew bastard" [*The Times* (London), 16 July 2000]
"f----- Jew b------" [UPI, 17 July 2000; euphemized *fucking* is one hyphen short]

"Jew bastard" [Reuters, 10, 16, 17 July 2000]
"Jew bastard" [*The Washington Post*, 18 July 2000]
"Jew bastard" [New York *Daily News*, 18 July 2000]
"Jew b------" [AP, 16 July 2000]

"an obscenity-laced, anti-Semitic slur" [AP, 19 July 2000]
"an anti-Semitic obscenity" [AP and *St. Louis Post-Dispatch*, 26 July 2000]
"hurled anti-Semitic abuse" [*The Times* (London), 18 July 2000]
"uttered an anti-Jewish slur" [Reuters, 16 July 2000]
"used an anti-Semitic slur" [AP, 16 July 2000]
"made an anti-Jewish remark" [*Time*, 24 July 2000, p. 64]
"used rough language" and an **"anti-Semitic slur."** [CBS Radio News, 16 July 2000]

~ ~ ~

The best book I have written, *Hillary Clinton's Pen Pal: A Guide to Life and Lingo in Federal Prison*, was suppressed by the "liberal" journalists for being too anti-Hillary and by their right-leaning tough-on-crime colleagues for being too pro-prisoners. Only one mainstream journalist wrote an intelligent front-page news story about it—only to be promptly ignored by his Clinton-loving colleagues and wire-service editors.

This prison primer is, of course, not just about what would happen to that quasi-criminal bitch if she were incarcerated. It is also a useful, life-saving guide for anyone facing prison-time. In addition, it provides an insider's account of how the inhumane Federal Bureau of Prisons and U.S. Department of Injustice and their goons operate.

While Hillary Clinton will not go to prison—where she belongs, together with her sleazy scumbag, Bill—because too many amoral morons keep paying for her $450-an-hour shysters, you can put her hypothetically in the slammer by reading my sarcastic and highly praised book.

FUCK AND *FUCKING*
THROUGHOUT HISTORY

"Scattered fucking *showers*, my ass." –Noah, 4314 BC

"How the fuck did you work *that* out?" –Pythagoras, 470 BC

"I don't suppose it's gonna fucking *rain*?" –Joan of Arc, 1431

"Where the fuck *are* we?" –Christopher Columbus, 1492

"You want *what* on the fucking ceiling?" –Michelangelo, 1508

"Where did all them fucking *Indians* come from?" –General Custer, 1876

"Any fucking *idiot* could understand that." –Albert Einstein, 1905

"Where is all this fucking *water* coming from?" –Captain Smith of the *Titanic*, 1912

"It does *so* fucking look like her!" –Picasso, 1922

"Where the fuck *am* I?" –Amelia Earhart, 1937

"Look at the *size* of this fucking gas bill!" –Adolf Hitler, 1944

"What the fuck was *that*?" –Mayor of Hiroshima, 1945

"Why? Because it's fucking *there*!" –Sir Edmund Hillary, 1953

"I need this parade like I need a fucking *hole* in my head." –John F. Kennedy, 1963

"Who's gonna fucking *know*?" –Richard Nixon, 1972

"That's not a *real* fucking gun." –John Lennon, 1980

"Let the fucking *woman* drive." –Commander of the *Challenger*, 1986

"It's a fucking *skin* condition! –Michael Jackson, 1992

"I *didn't* fucking do it!" –O.J. Simpson, 1994

"Aw, c'mon, Monica. Who the fuck is gonna find *out*?" –Bill Clinton, 1995

"Geez, I didn't think they'd get *this* fucking mad." –Saddam Hussein, 2003

Thanks to David Pressman and others. Dated & arranged by R.A.

FINNISH MALEDICTA
AND EUPHEMISMS

Helena Halmari

This article is an introduction to the most common "bad" words and their euphemisms in Finnish and a comparison with their English equivalents. There are relatively few Finnish swearwords and curses, consisting basically of four widely used and for Finns very strong and intensive expletives:

> **Helvetti!** *Hell!*
> **Jumalauta!** *God help!*
> **Perkele!** *Devil!*
> **Saatana!** *Satan!*

These terms are used independently as exclamations when one is angry. They are often preceded by the word **voi** ("oh"), are used as attributes to nouns: **helvetin ämmä** ("hell's old woman"), or as intensifying adverbs: **helvetin tyhmä** ("fucking stupid," "very stupid"), **saatanan hullu** ("Satan's crazy," i.e., "very crazy"). **Jumalauta!** can be used only as an interjection, not as an attribute of a noun, because syntactically it is an independent sentence ("God help!").

The above-mentioned four basic swearwords have proliferated a large number of euphemisms with various degrees of intensity, the connection with the original word being expressed in phonetic resemblance, mostly through alliteration (cf. English: *hell > heck, God > gosh, golly, devil > dickens, shit > shoot*, etc.).

1. HELL

The curse **Helvetti!** ("Hell!") has a number of euphemistic equivalents, many of which—like the euphemisms of other taboo or vulgar words—have no literal meaning:

Helkatti!
Helkkari!
Helkutti!
Helskutti!
Heikkari! (very mild)
Hiiskatti! (very mild)
Hiivatti! (very mild)

The phonological resemblance with the original word is quite remarkable—all the euphemistic forms start with the letter *h* and end in the letter *i*, and in all of them there are similar clusters of consonants in the middle. All consist of three syllables. Despite the apparent closeness to the original word, there is a huge difference in intensity. In addition to these milder forms of the word **helvetti,** there is a second group of words with the same phonetic characteristics, but these words are still milder than the preceding ones:

Himppu! "a little"
Himpsatti!
Himputti!
Himskatti!

These words are just mild expressions of annoyance. My five-year-old daughter uses **Himputti!** frequently, but I have not thought it necessary to try to root out this habit of hers, because the word is so harmless.

There are also a couple of other words starting with the letter *h*: **hiisi** and **hitto.** The translation of **hiisi** is either "hell" or "devil." The word usually does not occur alone but is used in the following expressions:

Painu hiiteen! *Go to blazes!*
Hiisi vieköön! *What the dickens!*
Lit., "(May) the Devil take!"

Hitto is also a mild curse and can, like **hiisi,** mean either "hell" or "devil." It is used in expressions like:

hiton hyvä *damn(ed) good*
Hitto soikoon (vieköön)! *Damn it! Hang it!*
Hell's bells! Lit., "Let the hell ring (take)!"
Mitä hittoa! *What the devil!*

The word **hitto** is still further euphemized to **hitsi**, which carries no connection to the meaning "hell"; the resemblance is simply phonetic, and it literally means "weld(ing)."

The word **horna** ("hell, abyss") belongs to the same group as **hiisi** and **hitto**. In everyday speech, this poetic word is used only in the exclamation **Painu hornan tuuttiin!** ("Go to the hell's gorge!")

2. DEITIES AND BLASPHEMIES

Jumalauta! ("God help!") quite surprisingly is used when one is really filled with anger. The word has lost most of its connections with the literal meaning, but it has kept its intensity. The following euphemistic interjections derived from it are fairly strong to medium. They are used when one is angry:

Jukolaut(a)!	**Jumalavita!**	**Jukupliut(a)!**
Jukoliut(a)!	**Jumaliut(a)!**	**Jumalaute!**
Jukravita!	**Jukoliste!**	**Jumaliste!**
Jukulaut(a)!	**Jukopliut(a)!**	
Jukuliuta!	**Jukraviti!**	**Amalauta!**
Juma! "God"	**Jukuliste!**	**Pirulauta!**

In addition to these euphemisms, there is a second group of fairly mild to very mild interjections derived from **jumalauta**. These euphemisms are used when one is astonished or surprised. They are used mainly by young schoolchildren:

Jukra!	**Jukupätkä!**
Jukranpuit!	**Jummi!**
Jukranpujut!	**Jumpe!**
Juku!	

The larger the phonetic differentiation between the original malediction and its euphemism, the milder the interjection becomes. This is the basic rule, although the connection with the original word is still clear. Usually, the first phoneme of the euphemism, here /j-/ or the first two /ju-/, are enough to maintain this connection.

There are several mild swearwords beginning with the letter *j* which, however, have no semantic connection with the word **jumalauta**. They are **juukeli** and **juupeli**, meaning "devil," but they are very mild and no longer used frequently. Also, the word **juutas** is quite obsolete; it means "Judas" (Iscariot), but the meaning today would be "deuce, devil."

3. DEVIL

The two basic, very intensive words are **perkele** and **saatana**, "devil" and "Satan," respectively. Both have a great number of more or less euphemistic equivalents. **Perhana** is quite close in intensity to the original word **perkele**, but there is a group of stronger and milder forms, all starting with the letter *p*:

Perhana! (very strong)	**Pentele!** (quite strong)
Perkale! (quite strong)	**Perkule!** (quite strong)
Persana! (quite strong)	**Peeveli!**
Peijakas!	**Peijooni!**
Perkiisi!	**Perskatti!**
Pirhana!	**Pirkale!**
Pirkele!	**Pirkule!**
Pirsana!	**Pirskatti!**

There are several other terms that have a fully "decent" literal meaning but are borrowed for the purpose of swearing mildly and avoiding the strong word **perkele**:

Perjantai! "Friday"
Permanto! "floor"

Because of the phonetic resemblance (the identical initial sounds /per-/) they are sometimes used as mild oaths.

∾

Abroad, the Finns are famous for their **Perkele!** because the Finnish phoneme /r/ is pronounced with a strong trill of the tongue, and thus the word **perkele** is quite audible, especially when pronounced in anger, as it is usually done. Equal in intensity to **Perkele!** is the curse **Saatana!** ("Satan!"), and it also has a number of milder forms:

> **Saakeli!** (quite strong)
> **Saamari!** (relatively strong)
> **Samperi!** (relatively strong)
> **Saakura!**
> **Saakuta!**
> **Saakuri!**
> **Saakutti!**
> **Saaplari!**
> **Saateri!**

When I was a child in the 1960s, there was a sentence which was felt to be a strong "no-no." It read: **Perhosia saatavana Helsingin torilla.** It means "Butterflies for sale at Helsinki marketplace," but because the first three words resemble the curses **perkele, saatana** and **helvetti**, the one who dared to utter the sentence was quite a daredevil.

Other euphemisms (many of which are already obsolete) meaning "devil" are:

beelsebuub "Beelzebub"	**belsebuub(i)**
pelsepuupi	**hornahinen** "small devil"
jeeveli	**juukeli**
juupeli	**kehveli**
lempo	**lemppari**
lempsatti	**paholainen**
pahus	**pannahinen**
piesa	**piru**
pirulainen	**sarvipää** "hornhead"
turkanen	

If we look at the meanings of these "basic" Finnish swearwords and curses, we can see that all are references to strong taboos: the devil, Satan, hell, and on the other extreme, God. In this respect, Finnish is similar to English. However, unlike their Finnish equivalents, the words *devil* and *Satan* are not strong swearwords in English. Further, the terms *God, God help* and *hell* are very much milder than their Finnish equivalents.

Despite their intensity, the above words are quite frequently used among speakers of Finnish. However, they have not lost any of their intensity through the centuries, although it seems that schoolchildren are quite a bit freer to use them nowadays, mostly as part of showing off. Adult use is still quite strongly restricted to male Finnish speakers, and these words are not felt to belong to cultured speech. Quite rarely can a woman be heard using these words in day-to-day life, and most of those who do use them are drunk when uttering them in public. (I must confess, however, that I have heard those words used by my innocent-looking schoolgirls after I had returned their English term papers with a low mark—a moment of ultimate grief and agony!) It is true that these days women do swear more than they used to—swearing by women is evidently seen as a verbal manifestation of equality between the sexes. The use of the above words is, however, generally regarded as vulgar.

4. OBSCENITIES

So far I have not mentioned the fifth "basic" Finnish swearword because it comes from another area of taboos, "indecent body parts." This word is **vittu** ("cunt"). This is the word most often heard in schoolyards in junior high schools. (There must be some truth to the Finnish proverb, *Siitä puhe mistä puute*, "One talks about what one lacks," although this word is used as frequently by girls as by boys.)

Again, there is a basic difference between Finnish and English concerning this word. One of our most frequently used exclamations is **Voi vittu!**, but I have never heard an English-speaking person exclaim "Oh, cunt!" in the sense of "Goddamn!" or "Jesus Christ!"

When it comes to the English swearword or intensifier

fucking, we lack this kind of usage altogether. (To Finns, "fucking" must be a positive thing!)

Although the female organ's name is frequently uttered when something goes wrong, the Finns never use the name of the corresponding male organ, **kulli** or **kyrpä** ("prick"), as an interjection expressing annoyance—what an area of language use for feminists to conquer!

Vittu is a strong, vulgar word, and thus it has given birth to rather mild, jocular interjections. These are expressions with only a phonetic resemblance to **vittu**:

> **Voi vinetto!** *Oh, vinetto!* (a type of red wine)
> **Voi vitjat!** *Oh, chains!*
> **Voi vitsi!** *Oh, joke!*
> **Viulut!** *Violins!*
> **Viunat!** (alcoholic drinks)

The ways of referring to the above-mentioned female organ are abundant, but besides **Voi vittu!** they are rarely used as oaths. The "worst" words are **vittu** and **pillu** (both "cunt"). The degree of vulgarity of these two words is about the same—in fact, people do not share a common opinion on the degree of strength of these two words. I think that **vittu** is stronger, while many insist that **pillu** is a far nastier word.

The following nursery words and 'endearing,' jocular words derive from **pillu**:

pimpeli	pimputti	pimppa
pimppi	pimppu	pimpsa

The jocular euphemism for **vittu** is **mirri** (literally, "pussy-cat"). This usage is similar to other languages that also use the equivalents of *cat* to designate both the animal and the vulva; for example, Russian *kot*, French *chatte*, and English *pussy*.

There are common verbs derived from **vittu**: **vittuilla** ("to be nasty"), **vituttaa** ("to feel angry, disgusted"), an adjective **vittumainen** ("mean, nasty"), and a noun **vitutus** ("the feeling of anger, a bad feeling").

The corresponding male organ to **vittu** is **kyrpä** ("prick, cock"). There are synonymous terms, **kulli** and **mulkku**, which are not quite as nasty as **kyrpä**, and a jocular term, **pissakraana** "urine tap."

The words **kyrpä** and **mulkku** are also used to mean "very nasty person," similar to English *prick*. Mild nursery terms are **pippeli, kikkeli,** and **kikuli.**

For testicles there is a mild, almost neutral colloquial word, **muna,** usually in the plural **munat** ("balls," lit. "eggs"). Other languages also use the equivalents of *eggs* as vulgar terms for testicles, e.g., Russian *jájca*, Spanish *huevos*, and German *Eier.*

If we move further back, we will come across the rear end, or arse, or ass, or whatever the English-speaking people prefer to call their derrières. Finnish terms are probably as abundant, starting from the worst, **perse.** This word has given birth to many colorful expressions:

> **antaa/jakaa persettä** "to give/deal ass" *to surrender (easily)*
> *to sexual intercourse*
> **kaikki on päin persettä** "everything is towards the ass"
> *everything has gone wrong*
> **nuolla persettä** "to lick somebody's ass" *bootlicking,*
> *brown-nosing*
> **repiä perseensä** "to tear one's ass" *to get mad, very angry*
> **olla perse auki** "to have the ass open" *to be (temporarily)*
> *without money*

The last expression has euphemistic forms, one using initials: **olla pee aa/p.a.,** and another where *perse* ("ass") is omitted: **olla auki** "to be open."

Euphemistic expressions referring to *arse*, some of which are derived from **perse** are:

> **pehva**
> **pemppu** (especially when talking to kids)
> **peppu** (especially when talking to kids)
> **perä** "rear"
> **persetti**
> **perskatti**

pylly
takamus "backside"
takapuoli "backhalf"
ahteri "bottom, rump, behind" (somewhat obsolete).

5. TERMS OF ABUSE AND INSULTING EXPRESSIONS

In Finnish, when you are mad at somebody, you either ask him *to smell something* or *to go somewhere*:

Haista vittu! *Smell the cunt!* (vulgar)
Haista paska! *Smell shit!* (vulgar, but milder than the preceding)
Haista home! *Smell mold/mildew!* (mild)
Haista kukkanen! *Smell the flower!* (very mild)
Painu vittuun! *Go to the cunt!* (vulgar)
Suksi vittuun! *Ski to the cunt!* (vulgar)
Painu helvettiin! *Go to hell!* (strong)
Painu helvetin kuuseen! *Go to hell's spruce tree!* (strong)

In English usage, there is no equivalent of **Painu vittuun!** ("Go to the cunt!"), nor is there in German (*Geh zur Fotze!*); in Russian, however, there is a similar expression, *Idí v pizdú!* "Go up a cunt!" (i.e., "Fuck off!") and a corresponding one using the male organ, *Idí na huj!* ("Go to the prick!")

One of the worst insults one can utter in Finnish is formed with **vittu** ("cunt"):

Vedä vittu päähäs! *Pull the cunt into your head!*

This is rivalled in nastiness by:

Työnnä sormi perseesees! *Push your finger into your ass!*

Further insulting expressions are **Vedä kätees!** and **Vedä kuivat!** Both mean "Masturbate!", "Go jerk off!" (lit., "Draw in your hand!" and "Draw dry ones!" or "Fuck dry!"). Russian has a corresponding term: *Ebat' v suhúju!* ("Fuck [it] dry!").

Pää ("head") is used in various insults:

kusipää "pisshead"   **munapää** "ballhead"
paskapää "shithead"

Other terms for body parts and excretions:

paskaperse "shitass"
perseenreikä "asshole"
kakka, paska and **skeida** "shit"
sonta "animal shit"
kusi, pissa and **virtsa** "urine"
pieru "fart"
perseensuti (strong) and **perssuti** (less vulgar)
"hair around the anus"

Vulgar English expressions formed with the word *mother* are not used in Finnish, and we do not have an expression corresponding to *motherfucker* or *Fuck your mother!* However, according to my high school students, it may be used as a literal translation from English: **Mee äitiäs nussiin!** ("Go fuck your mother!"), but this utterance is felt to be very taboo, and if used at all, it is a direct loan from English, not an original Finnish expression. English has influenced our language very much in the last years, also in the area of swearing. *Oh, shit!* may be heard more often than the Finnish equivalent **Voi paska!** and the expression *Fuck off!* is also commonly used among schoolchildren.

Well, as a language teacher I should probably be happy that *something* is said spontaneously in the foreign language!

SOURCES

Ailio, Pekka. "How to Swear in Finnish." April 1979. Unpublished manuscript. Maledicta Archives.

The Alternative Dictionaries. http://www.notam02.no/~hcholm/altlang/

Kauffman, Charles A. "A Survey of Russian Obscenities and Invective Usage," *Maledicta* 4 (1980): 261–289.

Nykysuomen sanakirja. 2nd ed. Porvoo: WSOY, 1980.

Petruck, Miriam. "Body Part Terminology in Finnish." Berkeley: University of California. May 1979. Unpublished manuscript. Maledicta Archives.

Razvratnikov, Boris S. (pseud.). "Elementary Russian Obscenity," *Maledicta* 3 (1979): 197–204.

Daily contacts in the schoolyard with Finnish children and adolescents.

ROMANI INSULTS

Edgar A. Gregersen

Maj feder te sines ma ekha suriasa "Better if you cut me with a knife" is a traditional Romani comment on an insult. Indeed, such an attitude (rather than the "Sticks and stones may break my bones but words will never harm me" sentiment expressed in English) is found in many other societies. Given this recognized importance it is unclear why verbal abuse has been little studied in general.

From my own preliminary examination of insult repertoires from round the world, it is clear that fairly obvious "insult topic areas" can be set up. For example, Japanese has no mother insults and practically no sexual insults of any kind, but its speakers often compare opponents to vegetables. Traditional Eskimo reveals no set insults of any kind. Eastern European languages have what I call "aggressive sexual insults" — on the order of "I fuk X", but these are not general in western European languages. North Africa (including southern Italy and extending thruout the Middle East) generally makes use of references to the sex organs of one's opponent's female relatives. And so on.

The insults used by Roma have to my knowledge never been examined in a systematic way. Earlier writers occasionally mention insults but largely to support some greater ethnographic objective. In the *Journal of the Gypsy Lore Society* there has not been a single paper devoted to the topic of verbal abuse in its many years of publication, tho particular insults are sometimes discussed. For example, in a 1931 article on Viennese Gipsies, Karl Otter states that:

Note: The author prefers to spell some words in his orthography.

73

The greatest insult to a Gypsy is to say to him "**Tu tscharaha ti rom-niaki mintsch**" [standard orthography: *Tu čaraha t'i romniaki minč* "You touched your wife's kunt"]. If a man were known to have done this, he would be subject to universal contempt, and excluded from all intercourse with the tribe. (p. 114; Emphasis, modern orthography, and translation added, EAG.)

Interestingly, Otter leaves the Romani expression untranslated—perhaps because he feels it would be too shocking in English. In a footnote, he notes a similar insult quoted in an 1880 work by V. Tissot, *Voyages au pays des Tziganes* (4th ed., Paris, p. 320): **Metschiwawa tiro schero tele tiri romniakri socha** [*me čivava tiro šero tele tiri romniakri šoxa* "I put your hand under your wife's skirt"]. This is also left untranslated. Both of these insults are unique in my cross-cultural corpus. How they could function as insults at all is not clear, but they are vaguely reminiscent of the Kiriwina form: **Kwoy um kwava!** "Copulate with your wife!", reported by Bronislaw Malinowski as perhaps the most serious of all insults among the Trobriand Islanders of Papua New Guinea (cited in his 1932 book *The Sexual Life of Savages*, London: George Routledge & Sons, p. 409).

An article by Irving Brown, "The Gypsies in America" (1929) mentions **phabulo čo baχt** [*phabulo čo baxt*] "A curse on your luck." Articles dealing with notions of ritual cleanliness may include references to words such as **moχadi** [*moxadi*] (or *mokadi* or *marime*) "unclean, defiled" but give no clue as to whether they can be used as insults as in some other languages (they seem not to be in Romani—at least at present). Dora E. Yates's 1930 discussion of tabus on mentioning the names of dead relatives and the extension of this tabu to words that are the same as or similar to such names (a custom sometimes referred to by the Zulu term *hlonipha*) does not specify if breaking such a tabu could be used in insults— as it reportedly is among the Yãnomamö of South America. (The example she gives is the girl's name Forella, which requires that the term *forelle* "trout" has to be changed to **mulo**

mādscho [*mulo mačo*] "the dead fish" or **lolo mādscho** [*lolo mačo*] "the red fish.*") However, Ian Hancock informs me that merely invoking the names of one's opponents dead relatives can be insulting—and indeed very serious, especially if one insults those relatives.

The most notable exception to not dealing with Gipsy insults is a 1979 article by F. David Mulcahy: "Studies in Gitano Social Ecology: Conflict and Verbal Abuse," which appeared not in the *Journal of the Gypsy Lore Society* but in *Maledicta*. In this article, Mulcahy wants to relate the symbolism of verbal abuse to a variety of "ecological niche theory" as envisaged by Donald L. Hardesty. The study deals not with Romani but with a Roma dialect of Spanish. One of the most striking points Mulcahy makes is that in Los Foros, the area occupied by Roma, is separated from the "Gentile" community by a kind of no-man's land. The extraordinary thing is (to quote Mulcahy) a "cultural pattern associated with this zone of separation [:] the habit of many of the Gitano children of defecating on its Gentile margins. This is done in daylight and in full view of the Gentiles" (p. 89). Mulcahy suggests that this symbolism is carried over into the insult system where the frame ¡Me cago en...! "I shit on...!," common enough in the Castilian Spanish phrases ¡Me cago en tu madre! "I shit on your mother" or ¡Me cago en Dios! "I shit on God!" and some variants of the two, has been expanded and elaborated on so that one finds:

¡Me cago en tu raza! I shit on your lineage race!
... en tu descedencia! ...on your whole line!
... en tu muertos! ...on your dead ones!
... en los cojones de tus muertos! ...on the balls of your dead ones! And so on.

My own study is considerably less symbolically oriented. As part of a project in part to map the insult areas of the world, I simply tried to find a native speaker of Romani who would be willing to report as much of the set insult repertoire that he could remember at the time of the interview. What I want is set insults—not secret ones—that any or most native speakers would know. An attempt to interview a speaker in Zagreb was aborted. Later, the late Mimi Kaprow said she would help, but in point of fact nothing came of it. One day in Manhattan, I noticed a number of men and women sitting outside a fortune-teller's shop. I approached the men and told them what I wanted. One of them said he would be willing to help me but when I tried to set up an appointment he was quite vague. In point of fact I never saw him again (altho this was not far from where I live). Some days later, I went to the same shop and asked the woman who was the resident fortune-teller when the man would return. She said that for $20 she would tell all the insults I wanted. I agreed but said I would have to go home to get my questionnaire and other materials. She apparently thought I had no money and started screaming at me for being a penniless bum. The insults were in English, not even in Romani.

Several fortune-tellers later (who denied that they or anyone they knew spoke Romani), I came upon another possibility: the neon sign advertised character readings on the second floor. I entered and at the top of the stairway a little girl soon appeared. I asked if anyone there spoke Romani. She said she did. I asked if I could speak to her father. She went into a room and a moment later an older woman appeared, apparently her mother. She wanted to know what I wanted. I was hesitant to ask her to be an informant because women much more often than men were appalled at my project. But fearing I had no other choice I tried to explain. After trying to be as clear but as inoffensive as possible, the woman looked outraged at me and said: "You want me to talk dirty to you? Get out before I get my husband to throw you down the stairs."

I got out.

Sometime later, I saw a young man and a somewhat older

woman sitting outside yet another fortune-teller's shop. I went up to the man and asked if he knew anyone who spoke Romani. It was the woman who asked why. I hesitatingly said that I needed some "translations." She continued to be curious and within a few minutes I told them more precisely about my project. She seemed amused when I mentioned the Japanese and Eskimo examples and was not offended in any way. And then she gave me the name of the person who would, she thought, be the ideal informant: John. But John was not in New York at the time and it was many weeks before he would come. Eventually, he did come and he agreed to be interviewed. The interview turned out to be one of the more interesting ones I had participated in.

The insults I collected were later converted into a standard spelling by Ian Hancock, who contributed four additional insults. The topics involved include:

1. aggressive sexuality (an Eastern European topic) e.g. **Kurrav kj'a da!** "I fuk your mother!"

2. "crazy vegetables" (also Eastern European) e. g. **Kolompìri dili** "crazy potato"

3. aggressive urination (fairly unique) e.g. **Mutrav ma pe kj'o muj!** "I pis in your mouth!"

4. mother insults e.g. **Mariv kj'a da!** "I defile your mother!"

5. various cross-culturally unusual insults e.g. **Te kurren pe le majmùja pe Tute!** "May the monkeys fuk you!" – **Džą te xas tj'a daki xin!** "Go eat your mother's shit!" – **Te xlen pe e lubnja ande tjire vàsura!** "May the whores shit in your crockery!" Reminiscent of the Spanish forms mentioned earlier, there is at least one reference to dead ancestors: **Kurrav ma pe kj'e mule** "I fuk your dead (ancestors)."

An insult apparently stressing submission rather than homosexuality is **Xa murro kar!** "Eat my kok!" the equivalent of "Suck my kok!", fairly common in the world's repertoires. Interestingly, as Ian Hancock has pointed out, a kind of reciprocal expression exists: **Xav tj'o kar!** "I eat your kok!", which means something like "I entreat you" or "please." We don't often find such reciprocal expressions—in English *"I kiss your arse" does not occur. But similar reciprocity images are found in a few other languages. Gimi, a language spoken in Papua New Guinea, is one—where the same phrase is used to express gratitude: "I eat your kok." In Tikopia, a Pacific Island language as reported by Raymond Firth, the gods are placated by worshipers who proclaim "We eat your shit," "We eat ten times your shit." Very little about such a reciprocity is known however, and Romani may be unique in that it extends the use of this frame "I eat..." for a number of other comparable entreaties: I eat your arse, liver, kunt.... Hancock wrote me that this used to be taken as proof of cannibalism among the Roma.

It would seem that Romani insults, at least in the (American) Vlax repertoire, fall within a basic Eastern European insult area. It would be interesting to find out how or if the repertoire of Romani speakers influenced by Turkish or other languages differs.

ADDENDUM

The following is the total corpus of insults elicited from my American Roma informant.

Kurrav kj'a da! "I fuk your mother!"
Kurrav ma pe kj'o muj! "I fuk your mouth!"
Kurrav ma pe kj'i baxt! "I fuk your luck!"
Kurrav ma pe kj'e mule! "I fuk your dead (ancestors)!"
Kurrav le Devleska da! "I fuk God's mother!"
Kurrav le beneska da! "I fuk the devil's mother!"
Mutrav ma pe kj'i baxt! "I pis on your luck!"
Mutrav ma pe kj'o muj! "I pis in your mouth!"
Mutrav ma pe kj'a dako muj! "I pis in your mother's mouth!"
Mariv kj'a da! "I defile your mother!"

Simtina diliyá "crazy semen/sperm/kum" [Hancock corrects *simtina* to *semìnci*; he suggests that the speaker seems to be using *smentìna*, which literally means "sour cream," but adds that this may be slang for "sperm."]

Bul diló "crazy arse" [Hancock corrects this form to *bul dili* and says the speaker has *bul* "arse" in the "wrong" gender: masculine, rather than the "correct" feminine.]

Banàna diló "crazy banana" [Again, Hancock corrects the gender and says the form should be *banàna dili*.]

Kresdevesto diló "crazy pickle/cucumber" [Hancock corrects *kresdevesto* to *krastevèco*.]

Kolompìdi dili "crazy potato" [Hancock corrects *kolompìdi* to *kolompìri* — I may have misheard the form.]

Kopìlčo "(male) bastard"

Kùrvo "whore"

Beštìjo "slut"

Xa murro kar! "Eat my kok!"

Džuvljorri "sissy" (lit. "little lady")

Te kurren pe le majmùne pe Tute! "May the monkeys fuk you!" [Hancock notes that *majmùne* is a regularized variant of *majmùja*.]

Tu san ekh gadžo "You're a gadjo [= non-Roma]."

Insults from other sources include the following: **Te xlen pe e lubnja ande tjire vàsura!** "May the whores shit in your crockery!" – **Dža te kurres tj'a da and'e bul!** "Go fuk your mother in the arse!" – **Me dem rril nùma e khand avili Tutar!** "I farted but the stink came from you!" – **Dža te xas tj'a daki xin!** "Go eat your mother's shit!" – **Xav ti dakeri minj!** "I eat your mother's kunt!"

ACKNOWLEDGMENTS

This paper is an expanded version of a talk given at the annual meeting of the Gypsy Lore Society, Florence, 1999 June 29. I am indebted to Professor Ian Hancock for all his help and to members of the conference for their comments.

QUOTES FROM AMERICAN ATHLETES

▶ Chicago Cubs outfielder André Dawson on being a role model: "I wan' all dem kids to do what I do, to look up to me. I wan' all the kids to copulate me."

▶ New Orleans Saints running back George Rogers, when asked about the upcoming season: "I want to rush for 1,000 or 1,500 yards, whichever comes first."

▶ Torrin Polk, University of Houston receiver, on his coach, John Jenkins: "He treats us like men. He lets us wear earrings."

▶ Football commentator and former player Joe Theismann, 1996: "Nobody in football should be called a genius. A genius is a guy like Norman Einstein."

▶ A senior basketball player at the University of Pittsburgh: "I'm going to graduate on time, no matter how long it takes."

▶ Bill Peterson, a Florida State football coach: "You guys line up alphabetically by height." And, "You guys pair up in groups of three, then line up in a circle."

▶ Lou Duva, veteran boxing trainer, on the Spartan training regime of heavyweight Andrew Golota: "He's a guy who gets up at six o'clock in the morning regardless of what time it is."

▶ Chuck Nevitt, North Carolina State basketball player, explaining to Coach Jim Valvano why he appeared nervous at practice: "My sister's expecting a baby, and I don't know if I'm going to be an uncle or an aunt."

▶ Shelby Metcalf, basketball coach at Texas A&M, recounting what he told a player who received four F's and one D: "Son, looks to me like you're spending too much time on one subject."

▶ Amarillo High School and Oiler coach Bum Phillips, when asked by Bob Costas why he takes his wife on all the road trips: "Because she is too ugly to kiss good-bye."

Pete Metzger and others submitted these jewels.

ANAL CUNT SONG TITLES

Reinhold Aman

Nathan Say alerted me to the American hard-metal/punk-rock band *Anal Cunt*, whose song titles are the most offensive ones I've seen and outdo the nasty rock-band names featured in *Maledicta 10*. The songs' lyrics, available on the Website listed below, match the titles in their offend-everyone spirit. From that band's songs (1996–2001), I've listed below an alphabetized sample of titles, some of which are actually black-humor-funny in their nastiness.

Because You're Old
Being A Cobbler Is Dumb
Being Ignorant Is Awesome
Body By Auschvitz
Dead, Gay And Dropped
Deadbeat Dads Are Cool
Domestic Violence Is Really Really Really Funny
Dumb, Fat and Gross
Even Though Your Culture Oppresses Women, You Still Suck You
    Fucking Towelhead
Ha, Ha Your Wife Left You
Hitler Was A Sensitive Man
I Became A Counselor So I Could Tell Rape Victims They Asked
    For It
I Convinced You To Beat Your Wife On A Daily Basis
I Fucked Your Wife
I Got An Office Job For The Sole Purpose Of Sexually Harassing
    Women
I Got Athletes Foot Showering At Mike's
I Hope You Get Deported
I Intentionally Ran Over Your Dog
I Just Saw The Gayest Guy On Earth
I Like Drugs And Child Abuse

I Lit Your Baby On Fire
I Made Fun Of You Because Your Kid Just Died
I Made Your Kid Get AIDS, So You Could Watch It Die
I Noticed That You're Gay
I Pushed Your Wife In Front Of The Subway
I Sent A Thankyou Card To The Guy That Raped You
I Sent Concentration Camp Footage To America's Funniest Home
    Videos
I Snuck A Retard Into A Sperm Bank
I Sold Your Dog To A Chinese Restaurant
I'm Glad You Got Breast Cancer, Cunt
I'm Not That Kind Of Boy
I'm Sick Of You
If You Don't Like The Village People, You're Fucking Gay
Jack Kevorkian Is Cool
Kill Women
Recycling Is Gay
The Only Reason Men Talk To You Is Because They Want To Get
    Laid, You Stupid Fucking Cunt
Van Full of Retards
Woman, Nature's Punching Bag
You Are An Interior Decorator
You Are An Orphan
You Can't Shut Up
You Converted To Judaism So A Guy Would Touch Your Dick
You Got Date Raped
You Look Adopted
You Look Divorced
You Robbed A Sperm Bank Because You're A Cum Guzzling Fag
You Rollerblading Faggot
You Were Too Ugly To Rape, So I Just Beat The Shit Out Of You
You're A Fucking Cunt
You're In A Coma
You're Old (Fuck You)
You're Pregnant, So I Kicked You In The Stomach
You've Got Cancer
You've Got No Friends
Your Kid Committed Suicide Because You Suck
Your Kid Is Deformed

Source: http://www.darklyrics.com/a/analcunt.html

SCATOLOGICAL FLYTING IN THE COLLOQUIES OF AELFRIC, SURNAMED "THE BAT"

David W. Porter

The medieval colloquy as a form or genre is easy to define. It is a conversational text designed to teach communication skills in a foreign language, namely Latin. The most famous example by far is that of Abbot Aelfric ("Grammaticus"), the writer whose work makes up the largest segment of the Anglo-Saxon prose corpus. Aelfric's colloquy was written in Latin and was designed to teach that language to English-speaking boys at about the turn of the millennium. One of those boys must have been Aelfric Bata, who calls Abbot Aelfric "my master." Like Abbot Aelfric, Bata ("the bat,"[1] ca. 995–1075) was a teacher who favored the colloquy for Latin instruction.

Bata's colloquies[2] are among the most outlandish medieval texts I have ever encountered. They are set in the eleventh-century monastic school and the characters in them are monks, usually teachers and students. Although one might expect religious content, these colloquies exhibit no evidence of a moral sense whatsoever. How to get ahead, to get what you want, whether it be food, a haircut, permission to leave the cloister at night, money for a manuscript-copying job—these are the things that Bata addresses. Arguments, which are a commonplace feature of colloquies, are carried to the furthest extreme in those of Bata. In one interchange the master and students bind a thieving boy and beat him well (pp. 61–63). When the victim pleads for mercy, the teacher urges those applying the rods to strike harder because "he doesn't feel a thing." When the victim claims that they are killing him, the master replies, "You're not dead yet."

In another interchange Bata intermingles scatological insults with the verses of the biblical book of Proverbs in almost the only example of ludic flyting from the Anglo-Saxon period (pp. 51–57). Here the interlocutors are apparently a master and a misbehaving student. The conversation begins *in medias res*, so we don't know the cause of the characters' hostility. The miscreant student's utterances, however, allow no mistake: he was a novice monk with an attitude, determined to give as good as he got.

Here is that colloquy. After a general condemnation of the student's evil ways, in which he calls the misbehaving student "a shit," the master says, here in English translation, except for one paragraph with the original Latin abuse:

Master: You little fox,[3] the seed of a demon, you flatter and seduce your fellows, and so do those who are like you, who agree with you—always wrongly encouraging toward evil and dragging others to evil and inviting envy of wrong deeds. No demon is worse than a son of discord or a murmurer among harmonious and peaceful people.

Student: You have power over me, my enemy. You can say whatever you wish about my poor self. What do you say against me?

Master: *Tu sochors!* You idiot! *Tu scibalum hedi!* You goat shit! *Tu scibalum ovis!* You sheep shit! *Tu scibalum equi!* You horse shit! *Tu fimus bovis!* You cow dung! *Tu stercus porci!* You pig turd! *Tu hominis stercus!* You human turd! *Tu canis stercus!* You dog shit! *Tu vulpis scibalum!* You fox shit! *Tu muricipis stercus!* You cat turd! *Tu galline stercus!* You chicken shit! *Tu asini scibalum!* You donkey turd! *Tu vulpicule omnium vulpiculorum!* You fox cub of fox cubs! *Tu vulpis cauda!* You fox tail! *Tu vulpis barba!* You fox beard! *Tu nebris vulpiculi!* You skin of a fox cub! *Tu vechors et semichors!* You stupid halfwit! *Tu scurra!* You buffoon! *Quid vis habere ad me?* What do you have for me? *Nihil boni autumo.* Nothing good, I'm sure.

Student: I would like you to be totally bepissed and beshat for all these words of yours. May you have shit in your beard! May you have shit in your beard, and shit and turds in your mouth, three and two times and eight and one and I none at all ever! Now your words show you to be a buffoon and a silly blabbermouth. When people come to you, you can do nothing better than beshit and befoul them with your shitty words and stupidities. I am not as smart as you are. I can in no way use wisdom; I don't know how in any degree, because I am too young.

Master: Why can't you do good like these others of our boys? Because you are wasting away and becoming less and shrinking and withering. May you always wane and never wax. May you always waste away and never thrive!

Student: Most stupid man, you always speak stupid words, stupidly changing your story back and forth. You speak maliciously, never kindly. You stupid evil one.

Master: You're a bad boy. Stop, you pitiful thing, stop! And stop acting so stupidly and wandering about. Young men die as old men. Think that this life quickly passes and that all temporal things are perishable and often are moved like the smoke of a fire in the face of the wind. We exist today—I don't know if we'll be alive tomorrow or not. Why won't you act right like this one does, my most beloved boy and dearest friend? He is not as old as you are but still he reads, sings, and speaks better and more correctly and more beautifully than you do. He is twelve years old, not more, but he's not a loudmouth like you who now carry 15 or 16 years on your back . You don't realize that wisdom in a youth is better than stupidity in an old man and that a boy of a hundred years of age[4] will be cursed. It will be well for you to speak to me wisely, boy.

Student: I don't care for your wisdom. I care nothing for your teaching or your admonition. My stupidity is my wisdom. Everyone is stupid before he is wise. Answer me according to my folly, since it is written: "Answer a fool according to his folly, lest (by chance) he be wise in his own conceit."[a] Wisdom and folly can never agree. And "he that reproveth a scorner"[b] (as I am) "getteth to himself shame, and he that rebuketh a wicked man getteth himself a blot."[c] Again, "reprove not a scorner, lest he hate thee"[d]; "rebuke a wise man and he will love thee."[e] "Give instruction to a wise man and he will be yet wiser."[f] "If thou be wise, thou shalt be a wise son for thy father's instruction"[g] but I am no so yet. "But a scorner" such as I am "heareth not rebuke."[h] And "go from the presence of a foolish man, when thou perceivest not in him the lips of wisdom."[i] "Wherefore is there a price in the hand of a fool to get wisdom, seeing he hath nor heart to it?"[j] "A reproof entereth more into a wise man than an hundred stripes into a fool."[k] "Even a fool, when he holdeth his peace, is counted wise."[l] Therefore, "a fool hath no delight in understanding, but that his heart may discover itself."[m] Speak to me according to my ignorance! This pleases me and this way we can be friends to one another and at the same time have friendship and hold harmony.

Master: Brother, believe me, I care neither for your friendship nor you enmity. Whether you are my friend or my enemy, I don't care.

Student: Nor do I. But I'll tell you one thing, whether you like it or not—wherever you are, may a beshitting follow you ever.

Master: I know one thing for certain, that "a fool is not brought up short by words, and he that spareth his rod hateth his son, he that loves his son brings him up short with a rod."[n] He rightly loves his student who beats him often. But the kind sympathy of the master often harms the boy.

Student: Are you going to threaten me like this all day? I don't care a bit for your teaching.

Master: Stop your words now, since the whips are ready.

What man, what kind of teacher, taught you to speak so stupidly? I never taught you to speak like that, nor any of our teachers. Where were you taught that you are such a great dullard? I don't think you were taught in this monastery. You set a bad example for our boys with your blabbering and shameful speech. But they shouldn't copy your language or teaching or foolishness. In fact I often correct you with words and punishment and whips and frequent warnings, but it does me no good. You won't do what I teach at all. I'll instruct you with words of wisdom according to my small learning. You get your folly from everywhere. You don't know that "the turning away of the simple shall slay them, and the prosperity of fools shall destroy them...."º

Here follows a long series of biblical proverbs. The colloquy then closes with an exhortation to choose the way of the wise and reject the way of the foolish.

The colloquies are the artistic production of an original, unconventional individual whose imagination and personality make themselves evident on every page. In the above example Bata has turned everything on its ear: the rigidly hierarchical relationship among members of the monastic community; the trope of the aged youth; the moral teaching of holy scripture. The flippant attitude toward scripture gibes poorly with the moral exhortation of the peroration, and I for one see the jocularity as characteristic of Bata; the pious mouthings seem an afterthought. After all, why put scatological vocabulary and the book of Proverbs into the same lesson?

Near the close of the colloquies Bata justifies his use of the outrageous (p. 64): "As you learn in this lesson and read in many places, joking is often mixed and connected with the words and pronouncements of wisdom. For this reason I've made and arranged in my way this lesson for you young men. I know that boys speaking to one another in their way more often say words that are playful than wise or honorable. This age group with its naughty garrulity always uses foolish speech and frequent joking. They prefer to play and joke foolishly with their mates and this makes them very happy."

I have no doubt that Bata was an effective teacher. By memorizing the flyting episode translated above, for example, the student would have gotten valuable practice in the communicative task of giving insults, would have learned a good deal of holy scripture, and would have mastered perhaps the most important set phrases in medieval Latin, the maxims from Proverbs. And it is difficult to imagine students being inattentive—more likely they would have vied for the rôle of the misbehaving student! But however much Bata may justify his unconventional method, he throws himself into it so enthusiastically that I detect a gratuitous delight in the violation of social custom.

What a contrast Bata makes with his master. In the colloquy of Abbot Aelfric students took the roles of different professions such as hunting, fishing, or carpentry, and then argued about who gave the greatest benefit to society. That work was a sophisticated piece of instruction in language and in social and moral principles as well.[5] Bata on the other hand enjoys the rents in the social fabric. In his colloquies the characters are proponents of mercenary self-interest. The glass of beer procured, the stolen apples hidden away, the beating escaped, these are his concerns. He tells us he is Aelfric the Bat, "the shortest of monks." It is easy to imagine the diminutive eccentric in his black Benedictine robe flapping down the corridors of the monastery, watchful for opportunities of self-aggrandizement. In the only mention of Bata outside his own work, *The Life of St Dunstan* by Osbern,[6] we learn that he tried to disinherit the church of god but was prevented when St. Dunstan returned from beyond the grave to oppose him. Bata is a fascinating character indeed.

NOTES

1. Both Stevenson and Garmonsway ("The Development of the Colloquy") accept *Bata* as meaning "bat." Brooks (*The Early History of the Church of Canterbury*) suggests that the name means "the improver."

2. Bata's colloquies are found in *Early Scholastic Colloquies*, edited by W. H. Stevenson (Oxford: Anecdota Oxoniensis, 1929), pp. 27–74.

3. Here (and later in the conversation) "fox" apparently meant, as in modern English, a sly person and so was not a totally pejorative epithet. In the *vercelli* book there is a marginal note reading "Aelfmer the fox will thrash the boy Aelfric."

4. This is a fractured commonplace—the usual medieval trope praises young men who have the wisdom of old men. Cf. Ernst Curtius, *European Literature and the Latin Middle Ages* (N.Y.: Pantheon), pp. 98–101.

5. Anderson, Earl R. "Social Idealism in Aelfric's *Colloquy*," *Anglo-Saxon England* 2 (1973), 153–162.

6. *Acta Sanctorum*, May 19.

SCRIPTURAL CITATIONS

a. Proverbs 25:5   f. Prov. 9:9   k. Prov. 17:10
b. Prov. 9:7   g. Prov. 9:12   l. Prov. 17:28
c. Prov. 9:8   h. Prov. 8:1   m. Prov. 18:2
d. Prov. 1:7   i. Prov. 14:7   n. Prov. 13:24
e. Prov. 9:8   j. Prov. 17:16   o. Prov. 1:32

CHIDING CHINESE
CHILDREN-CHIDERS

Below are some sentences banned in 2001 by the Chaoyang District Education Committee in Beijing. The list was obtained by Robert Marquand, Beijing bureau chief of the *Christian Science Monitor*. Teachers are no longer allowed to say to their pupils:

You are slow and stupid.
The sight of you makes me sick.
Whoever teaches you has the worst of luck.
You are just simply an idiot.
Have your mother take you for a checkup—to test if you are
  retarded.
You are hopeless and incurable; no medicine can save you.
Sit down, stupid; don't raise your hand unless you know the right
  answer.
Shut up, I don't want to hear you.
You are the worst.
Retard.
Get out of here.
I believe you will have no future.
You are only a wood post with two ears.
You are a stick of elm that will never understand.
Dead fish keep their mouths shut.
You don't understand human speech.
Stupid, you just can't learn anything.
You are so stupid you need to check your I.Q.
How can you be so lazy, like a pig?
You only fill your stomach and daydream; you can do nothing but
  eat and you are hopeless.
I would have killed myself long ago if I were you.

Source: *Harper's Magazine*, Aug 2002, p. 23. Thanks to Eva H. (R.I.P.)

ETHOPATHY
A Word Whose Time Has Come

Joseph S. Salemi

This article announces a new coinage in English vocabulary. It provides the etymology, definition, and pronunciation for the proposed word and its derivatives, along with a brief account of the reasons why the coinage has become necessary. It is difficult for lexical innovations to win acceptance, and that is as it should be. English, like every fully developed language with a canon of literature behind it, has a more than sufficient vocabulary stock for all common purposes. Apart from specialized terms for new inventions or advances in technology, a language has little need to come up with neologisms. This is especially the case when speech addresses ordinary day-to-day existence and the perennial patterns of human interaction. We do not require new words for *love, hate, jealousy, friendship,* or *exploitation,* since the old ones do just fine. In fact, one mark of an inadequate writer is the urge to create artificial or nonce terms rather than make use of the perfectly functional vocabulary inherited in his native tongue. The habit of coinage might even be called infantile in the strict sense—a writer with a penchant for verbal novelties is like a baby learning to talk, who babbles out hybridized solecisms in his attempt to express meaning.

Having said this, it is also fair to point out that occasionally a coinage or neologism is not only appropriate but even demanded by a new condition or situation. Words like *brainwash, ideology, alienation,* and *genocide* were all created to address specific developments of modern life that, while not absolutely new, became peculiarly potent presences in the twentieth century. These realities loomed large, so we fashioned the words to name them.

Another reality hangs over our world, and it has gone nameless for too long. I have watched this evil thing gain power and momentum over the last thirty years, and although some observers have commented on and even condemned its various symptoms, no one has yet recognized that these symptoms are all manifestations of a common pathology. This pathology is running through society with a truly pandemic speed and virulence, and yet precisely because it is so widespread it has escaped general notice and attention. Like the air we breathe, it is now a condition of existence that no one ordinarily thinks about. The pathology has fostered a habit of mind so rootedly inveterate in millions of persons that *not* to be in its grip is often remarked upon as a sign of oddness or eccentricity.

The thing that I am talking about is *ethopathy,* and that is the term I have coined to name it. Let me begin attributively, by giving the characteristics of ethopathy.

Ethopathy is a state of mind or a personal disposition that is marked by a profound need to do something stupid, indecorous, or palpably absurd out of an unshakable emotional conviction as to its necessity. A telltale symptom of ethopathy is a desperate desire to be *au courant,* fashionable, and trendy —even if chasing these things means gross discomfort, ruinous expense, and personal abasement. Another infallible sign of ethopathy is a kind of frantic restlessness and disquiet that drives one to pursue idiotic courses of behavior with a tenacity that disregards all reasonable limits, *as if one's very life depended on acting like a total fool.*

Here are fifteen examples of ethopathic behavior:

▶ A housewife who subsists on tasteless, low-caloric food out of a desperate fear of gaining weight as she grows older is suffering from *ethopathy.*

▶ A high-level executive who ruins his health and his personal finances to snort cocaine, not because he likes it but because he wants to be accepted in a peer group that does so, is suffering from *ethopathy.*

▶ A man who, while not the victim of any debilitating psychic disorder, nevertheless spends large chunks of his free time and discretionary income going to mental therapy sessions is suffering from *ethopathy*.

▶ Apartment-bound urbanites who buy expensive and improbably contrived devices to exercise on for endless hours in their living rooms are suffering from *ethopathy*.

▶ A middle-class teenager who disfigures her body with tattoos and bizarre piercings out of a need to look like a *déclassé* punk-rock groupie is suffering from *ethopathy*.

▶ Persons who go to operas, concerts, ballets, and museums not for their personal enjoyment but simply to be perceived by others as "cultured," are suffering from *ethopathy*.

▶ A health-obsessed neurotic who runs out to buy a new vitamin pill after seeing it hyped in the *Science Times* as something wonderful is suffering from *ethopathy*.

▶ Women who insist on being trained as firemen, paratroopers, and fighter pilots just as a way of making some ideological point are suffering from *ethopathy*.

▶ Moralistic types who obsess about other people's use of drugs, alcohol, prostitutes, or pornography, and who go to extraordinary lengths to make sure that these people are prosecuted by the law, are suffering from *ethopathy*.

▶ An English professor who destroys his students' natural love of literature by forcing them to read jargon-clotted and tendentious literary theory is suffering from *ethopathy*.

▶ Persons who are constantly trumpeting their status as "victims" of abuse, neglect, maltreatment, oppression, or discrimination, and who then demand special treatment or indulgence because of it, are suffering from *ethopathy*.

▶ Hypersensitive types who rush out of the room when they catch a whiff of cologne or cigarette smoke, and then make accusatory whines about pulmonary dangers, are suffering from *ethopathy*.

▶ A yuppie poseur who ostentatiously uses a cellular phone in public places as a means of impressing strangers is suffering from *ethopathy*.

▶ A computer nerd whose eyes turn large and liquid while he rhapsodizes about the newest processor is suffering from *ethopathy*.

▶ A young man who walks the streets with a tape-player plugged into both ears so that not a spare second will go by without pop music passing through his head is suffering from *ethopathy*.

I could go on forever giving examples of ethopathy, but it is now time to generalize inductively. In every one of these cases, the person suffering from ethopathy evinces a devotion to a bizarre, ritualized behavior pattern that strikes non-ethopathic persons as meaningless or beside the point. And yet the sufferer can under no circumstances be made to see that his behavior is sick; he will have a powerful sense of the moral correctness of his actions, and of the obligation to behave as he is doing regardless of personal discomfort or untoward consequences.

At base ethopathy is a religious impulse, although ethopaths will adduce countless "rational" reasons why one should exercise incessantly, or pop nutrient pills, or find one's "inner child," or buy the latest and most uselessly complex computer. This religious impulse has no specific divinity as an object, but it manifests the same awe, dread, and terror that are part of the original semantics of the word *religio* in Latin. Ethopaths do what they do for two crucial reasons: they think they *ought* to do it, and they are afraid *not* to do it. Many ethopaths are secularists and worldlings, but in regard to their pet obsessions they behave exactly like frightened animists who will do anything to placate a fetish-idol or a sorcerer.

The deeply religious nature of ethopathy can be seen in the following series of quotations, which I report precisely as I have heard them spoken over several years. I have correlated the quotes with the religious attitudes that they illustrate.

Religious Attitude	Ethopathic Quotations
Solicitude for precisely performed rituals:	"You have to take exactly six different vitamin supplements." "It's essential to do fifty deep knee bends each morning."
Horror at acts of profanation:	"Oh my God, not red meat!" "How dare you blow secondary smoke while my children are here?"

Religious Attitude	Ethopathic Quotations
Humorlessness:	"I don't find sexist jokes like that to be funny, mister!" "Why are you laughing at my new ten-billion megabyte PC?"
Dependence on groupthink:	"But no one is eating refined sugar anymore!" "People won't sit with you at the lunch table if you say things like that."
Flagrant superstition:	"They say that this new South American vegetable extract can regenerate dead brain cells!" "My computer has definitely improved my prose style."
Use of arcane language:	"Group therapy sessions will help you reconstitute those interactive skills in personal relationships that past psychic trauma may have caused to atrophy." "Marxist and other post-imperialist critiques allow us to deconstruct the racist and colonialist substructures of the patriarchal canon."
Invidious distinction between the damned and the elect:	"Smart people eat macrobiotic meals exclusively." "The decent, humane, and caring segment of the population supports animal rights."

Religious Attitude	Ethopathic Quotations
Hunger for conversion experience and exalted states:	"I used to be cynical like that, but going through Primal Scream restored my faith in positive thinking." "You can't believe the high you get from sustained jogging!"
Adulation of gurus:	"Nobody really understood the nature of literature until Derrida came along." "Sally Jessy Raphaël saved my life."

Another sign of ethopathy's religious foundation is its intolerance of any intellectual questioning of its received tenets. Religion rests on powerful emotional reflexes that go far deeper than discursive argument. Indeed, arguing with ethopaths over their obsessive symptoms is mostly useless, and often dangerous. Try to convince a middle-aged secretary that driving thirty miles a day on her stationary bicycle will not appreciably enhance her marriage prospects or her lifespan, and be prepared for an explosion. Tell a yuppie twit that spending half his salary to live in Chelsea or Soho is patently insane when he could dwell cheaply and more comfortably in a nontrendy neighborhood, and he'll punch you out. Explain to a computer geek that the only tools one needs to write are paper, pen, and perhaps a typewriter, and he'll glare at you in pitying contempt. In each case the ethopath is impervious to rational appeals, and doggedly sticks to the True Faith with all the stubbornness of a Breton peasant.

Consider the vegetarian freak who makes a scene at a restaurant over the presence of animal fat in his dessert. Or the environmentalist fanatic who stops a major dam's construction to save some obscure snail species. Or the fundamentalist busybody who threatens a boycott of the local 7-Eleven because it carries *Playboy* magazine. Each of them is sick in a different way, but they have in common an ironclad devotion to an absurdity, and a need to live out the consequences of that absurdity regardless of their own discomfort and inconvenience or that of other persons. The modern world is infested with these infantile whiners, who make their own lives and the lives of those around them miserable. Our lexicon needs the word *ethopathy* to pin down, once and for all, the shared psychic disorder that unites all these various pathologies. After the disease has been recognized and named, we can begin to research its etiology and possible cure.

Someone might say: "These people are just silly and self-absorbed—we don't need a new word for their behavior." I say we *do* need a new word, because silliness and self-absorption have become so ubiquitous and unremarkable today that we have lost all sense of their pathological abnormality. Since the 1960s, our worship of the bogus ideals of "authenticity" and "self-fulfillment" has led us to accept as valid a whole range of modes of behavior and courses of action that a century ago would have been recognized as patently lunatic. A friend tells you that she's spending several thousand dollars to pass the summer at a health spa, where she'll be kept to a macrobiotic diet and a spartan regimen of exercise, *and no one laughs out loud*. Someone else announces that, at the age of forty-two, she's decided to take singing lessons and try for a career in opera, *and nobody tells her to sober up and stop dreaming*. An acquaintance asserts that a new self-help book put out by Simon and Schuster and hyped on the Oprah Winfrey show really contains the key to total human happiness, *and none of us advise him to get his head examined*. In the not-too-distant past, a community of family, friends, and neighbors would have laughed such propositions into oblivion—today we have all been conditioned to receive them as legitimate options and possibilities.

It might be objected that ethopathy is simply a form of mass hysteria and mindless me-too-ism manifesting itself in a range of predictable, politically correct lifestyle choices. However, ethopathy should be distinguished from mere faddiness and craze-mongering. An ephemeral fashion that sweeps society, such as hula hoops, bellbottom trousers, or cornrowed hair is not necessarily ethopathic or even harmful. These are just momentary enthusiasms that come and go, no different from imperial Rome's passion for steam baths or eighteenth-century France's predilection for powdered wigs. No one takes such fads seriously, not even the people who enjoy them. Ethopaths, however, take what they do very seriously. The thing that differentiates an ethopathic obsession from a modish vagary is psychic compulsion rooted in a crypto-religious mandate. Hair styles and skirt lengths are ultimately insignificant—they are based on nothing more important than the caprice of some couturier. But feeding oneself on hideous health food, or paying thousands to some quack therapist, or spending endless hours on a treadmill, or ranting about sexist pronouns, or piercing one's tongue with a silver stud, or getting apoplectic over pornography, or hounding cigarette smokers out of the room, or speaking deconstructionist jargon, *are all more than fads*: they are pathological infatuations based on what in German would be called a *Geistesstörung*—that is, a mental disorder. And unlike fads, these ethopathic disorders have a pernicious effect on society at large, for those in their grip believe passionately that what they are doing is virtuous and proper, and hence prescriptive for others.

Leisure time and a lot of discretionary income make ethopathy possible, plausible, and of course profitable to the array of institutions and corporations that thrive on its continued growth. The number of commercial concerns that are enriched by the spread of ethopathic delusions is legion: publishing conglomerates, drug companies, computer firms, health food stores, hordes of lawyers and physicians, exercise equipment manufacturers, New Age religions, major foundations, the electronic media, governmental bureaucracies, extensive strata of print journalism, and most of all that festering core of ethopathy, the American university. All of these profitable businesses grow in power and wealth as ethopathy infects more and more individuals, and naturally they have a vested interest in seeing the pathology prosper. In fact, an economic history of the last three decades could be written just researching the ways in which American corporations and their academic toadies have fostered the spread of lucrative ethopathic disorders such as vitamin obsession, avant-garde posturing, health food mania, fake art, computer worship, multiculturalism, therapy fads, and self-help quackery.

In a society where most persons had to work vigorously to make a living, none of the above-mentioned absurdities would have a chance to develop. Affluent, highly advanced cultures such as those of Western Europe and North America are the petrie dishes wherein ethopathy grows and flourishes. One does not normally find ethopathy in places like rural China, equatorial Africa, or the Amazon basin, where persons must still maintain a certain balance and sanity in order to survive the struggle for existence. However, as other parts of the globe begin to attain levels of development comparable to the West, we can expect the disorder to break out in full force there.

For all these reasons, a coinage is necessary—one whose very novelty will force us to see the increasingly sick behavior patterns around us with a renewed awareness of their absurdity and *bizarrerie*. That word is *ethopathy* and its derivatives, the etymology of which I shall now address.

The first part of the word *ethopathy* derives from the Greek noun ἦθος (*ethos*), which means the manners, habits, disposition, and character of a person. A man's ethos is the sum of his defining patterns of behavior, the things that he does and says which give an indication of his innermost essence. The word has been borrowed directly into English with little change of meaning, though in English *ethos* is generally used in reference to a nation, a cultural group, or a movement rather than to an individual.

I use the prefix *etho-* to mean patterns of behavior. This needs no explanation, as it is in conformity with related borrowings from the Greek such as *ethics* and *ethical*.

The second part of the word comes from the Greek noun πάθος (*pathos*), a word arising from the verb πάσχειν (*paschein*) with an aorist infinitive παθεῖν (*pathein*). This verb means to suffer, to endure, to receive an impression from without, to be the passive object of another's action. All derive from a Proto-Indo-European *kwenth-, which meant to suffer. *Pathos* in Greek can mean suffering, passion, or feeling. This word has also been borrowed directly into English, but in our language the word has come to mean the quality that arouses pity or sympathy, or those feelings themselves, and it tends to be used only in a literary context.

I use the suffix *-pathy* to mean sickness or disorder. Here some explanation is necessary.

The use of the suffixes *-pathy* and *-path* to create nouns has gone in three distinct directions in the history of English word-formation. This is due to the multiple semantics of the Greek noun *pathos*, which can mean suffering, passion or feeling. Moreover, since all these meanings have in common the notion of heightened perception, this fourth idea is also noticeable in some *-pathy* derivatives.

In words like *telepathy* and *telepath*, the idea of perception dominates. Telepathy is perception across barriers or distances without instruments; a telepath is a person capable of such perception. But in the word *empathy*, the idea of feeling is central to the term's semantics. Empathy is a deep understanding of another person's feelings and thoughts, marked by a closeness that allows one to share in them. An *empath* (the term is rare) would be someone skilled in this sort of understanding.

However, in words like *psychopath, neuropath,* and *sociopath*, the idea of suffering or sickness is primary. A psychopath is a deeply disturbed and deranged lunatic, often dangerously violent, who suffers from a severe mental disorder. A neuropath is someone suffering from a nervous condition. And a sociopath is someone suffering from a serious inability to adapt to the norms of human companionship and behavior. *Psychopathy, neuropathy,* and *sociopathy* are the respective conditions that blight the lives of these persons.

By a curious twist, *-pathy* and *-path* sometimes also mean the treatment of the diseased condition, and the doctor who treats. Thus *osteopathy* is the analysis and treatment of various bone disorders, and the *osteopath* is the doctor who specializes in this field. *Homeopathy* and *homeopath* conform to the same pattern. It may very well be, however, that a noun like osteopath is really a shortened form of *osteopathologist.*

In any case, the proposed neologisms *ethopathy* and *ethopath* are modelled on those existing words where the idea of suffering and sickness predominates. Hence an *ethopath* (like a psychopath or a sociopath) is a person afflicted with a disorder, and *ethopathy* is the name of that disorder. *Ethopathic* is the normally derived adjective, but it may also be used substantively, on the pattern of adjectives such as *anorectic* and *lunatic.* Thus *ethopath* and *ethopathic* can be synonyms.

The adverb *ethopathically* is also a natural development in this same series.

Are these terms maledictive? This is hard to answer. All words that refer to an intrinsically unpleasant reality tend to become pejoratives in the course of time. A word like *neurotic* began as a perfectly neutral description of a psychic condition, and can still be used as such, but today it is often maledictive in its connotations, e.g., *I won't work for that damned neurotic.* The word *retarded,* when referring to mental disability, was originally just a descriptive term; today it is almost always a pejorative and is therefore avoided by the medical profession. The sentence *What are you, retarded or something?* is now frightfully maledictive. So too, the coinages *ethopathy* and *ethopath* may start out as purely taxonomic, but I am certain that in the eventuality of their being accepted into our lexicon they will soon become useful and effective pejoratives. And we can expect to hear sentences like "You're a goddamned ethopath!" or "What kind of ethopathic insanity is this?" or "He's the most flagrant example of ethopathy since Michael Jackson."

~

The pronunciation guide and proposed definitions for the coinage *ethopathy* and its derivative forms are presented below. Each definition is followed by a usage sample, and pronunciation is given in common dictionary pronunciation rendering and IPA transcription.

PRONUNCIATION GUIDE

Standard English Orthography	Dictionary Pronunciation Rendering	IPA Transcription
ethopathy	ē thŏp' ə thē	iˈθɑpəθi
ethopath	ē' thō păth	ˈiːθopæθ
ethopathic	ē thō păth' ĭk	iθoˈpæθɪk
ethopathically	ē thō păth' ĭk lē	iθoˈpæθɪkli

Definitions

ethopathy *noun* **1.** a systematic pattern of disorder in a human being's behavior or way of life, manifesting itself in one or more varying forms of delusion, obsession, or absurd trend-chasing. *Usage sample*: Ethopathy is rampant in North America. **2.** any particular manifestation of this disorder, such as dieting, careerism, mindless exercise, multiculturalism, psychobabble, animal-rights activism, pharmaceutic addiction, gadget-worship, and the like. *Usage sample*: Worshipping one's computer is a common form of ethopathy.

ethopath *noun* a person suffering from any one of the forms of ethopathy. *Usage sample*: It is a mark of the ethopath to have no inner direction.

ethopathic *adjective* pertaining or relating to ethopathy or ethopaths. *Usage sample*: It is an ethopathic delusion to believe that vitamins are a panacea.

ethopathic *noun* a synonym for ethopath. *Usage sample*: Academia and health-spas are filled with ethopathics.

ethopathically *adverb* in a manner appropriate to ethopathy or ethopaths. *Usage sample*: Her politically correct euphemisms showed that she was ethopathically inclined.

DUTCH TERMS OF ABUSE

Carla van der Waal

T his article is an introduction to current Dutch terms of abuse, all meaning "unpleasant, despicable, nasty person" (i.e., not based on appearance, character or background).

EXAMPLES OF SIMPLE INVECTIVES

MALE
ellendeling (lit., wretched one)
hufter scoundrel
kwal (lit., jellyfish)
ploert cad
schoft scoundrel

MALE / FEMALE
naarling (lit., horrible one, repulsive one)
mispunt (lit., a missed point [at playing billiards])
stuk ongeluk (lit., piece of unhappiness / bad luck / accident)

FEMALE
kreng nasty piece of work (lit., carrion)
loeder nasty woman (lit., lure)
teef (lit., bitch, female dog)

The majority of invectives, however, are derived from the following three categories:

       1. Genitalia
       2. Serious diseases
       3. Bodily functions

Some words from these categories can be used on their own (marked with an asterisk). Most are used to construct "compound invectives," the stronger form of Dutch abuse. Compound invectives consist of strings of nouns in which the final noun is modified by one or more preceding adjectival nouns.

1. GENITALIA

a. Male Genitalia

bal* testicle (lit., ball; abbreviation of teelbal = testicle), on its own mostly used as invective meaning snooty type, e.g. **corpsbal** = fraternity member

eikel* glans (lit., acorn)

kloot* testicle (lit., ball) ; adjective: **klote** (= bad)

klootzak* scrotum (lit., ball sack)

lul* penis (dick, prick, cock)

pik* penis (dick, prick, cock)

zaadbal* testicle (lit., sperm ball)

zak* scrotum (lit., sack)

b. Female Genitalia

kut* vagina, vulva (cunt)

trut* vagina, vulva (also used as a goodhearted invective)

schaamlip* labium (lit., shame lip)

2. DISEASES

kanker cancer

k(o)lere cholera

pest plague

pleuris (short for *pleuritis*) pleurisy

pokken smallpox

schurft scurvy

takke attack, stroke (from the French *attaque*)

tering consumption, tuberculosis

tyfus typhoid

3. BODILY FUNCTIONS

bloed blood

darm* intestine

drek dung

etter* pus; *etteren* to act annoyingly

etterbuil* abscess (lit., pus boil)

gal gall

kak shit

klier* gland; *klieren* to act annoyingly

kots vomit

schijt shit

sekreet* secretion

stront shit

vet fat
zeik piss; *zeiken* to nag (lit., to piss)

CONSTRUCTING THE COMPOUND INVECTIVE

Nouns that can be used as an adjectival noun:
     kloot
     kut
     trut
     all nouns from category 2
     all nouns from category 3

Kut and **klote** are also used as adjectives referring to other things than persons (**kloteweer, kutweer** = bad weather; lit., "balls weather," "cunt weather") and as exclamations: **Kut! Klote!**

Adjectives often used in combination with invectives:
gore dirty
stinkend stinking; in compound invectives: **stink**
verrotte rotten; in compound invectives: **rot**
vieze dirty
vuile dirty

Use of multiple adjectives with the same meaning gives the invective more strength: e.g., **vuile vieze gore klootzak**

Most Common Final Nouns of Compound Invectives:

MALE
bak container, bucket; referring to face (*bakkes* = mug)?
hond dog
lul dick, prick, cock
nek neck
vent guy
zak scrotum

FEMALE
griet girl (vulgar, often derogatory)
hoer whore (not necessarily referring to behavior)
kut vagina, vulva
meid girl (vulgar, often derogatory form for *meisje*)
mens person; often derogatory form for "female"

teef (lit., bitch)
trut vagina, vulva
wijf woman (derogatory), broad
MALE / FEMALE
lijer (from *lijder*) sufferer
straal ray, jet, stream

CHILD
jong young one, kid

Some Examples of Common Compound Invectives
With Their Literal Translations

MALE
bloedbak blood bucket
boerenlul peasant dick
droplul licorice dick
etterbak pus bucket
galbak gall bucket
hondenlul dog prick
kloothommel testicle bumblebee
kotsnek puke neck
kutlul cunt prick
kwallenbak jellyfish bucket
lul de behanger prick the paperhanger
paardenpik horse cock
rotvent rotten guy
rotzak rotten scrotum
soeplul soup prick
teringhond consumption dog
tyfushond typhoid dog
vetnek fat neck
zakkenwasser scrotum washer, sack washer
zeikvent piss guy

FEMALE
boerentrut peasant cunt
kleremeid cholera girl
kut met vingers cunt with fingers
kut op wielen cunt on wheels
kutwijf cunt broad
pokkewijf smallpox broad

rotgriet rotten girl
rotmens rotten person
soepkut soup snatch
spinaziekut spinach twat
takkewijf stroke broad
teringhoer consumption whore
teringwijf consumption broad
turbotrut turbo cunt
tyfusteef typhoid bitch

MALE / FEMALE
etterstraal pus stream
kankerlijer cancer sufferer
lamstraal weak stream (of piss?)
rotstraal rotten stream
stuk stront piece of shit, turd
teringlijer consumption sufferer
zeikstraal piss stream

CHILD
etterjong pus kid
klerejong cholera kid
rotjong rotten kid
takkejong stroke kid
pestjong plague kid

Note: The more adjectival nouns preceding the final noun, the stronger the compound invective; e.g., **pestpokkentyfusteringkankerwijf**.

BIBLIOGRAPHY

Heestermans, Hans. *Luilebol! Het Nederlands Scheldwoordenboek.* Amsterdam: Thomas Rap, 1989
Laps, Kristiaan. *Nationaal scheldwoordenboek.* Amsterdam: Ploegsma, 1984
van Lichtenvoorde, Marnix en Marjan. *Scheldwoorden van de jaren negentig.* Helmond: Michon, 1993

CITY OF NEW YORK

REVISED HIGH SCHOOL
MATH PROFICIENCY EXAM

NAME _____ GANG NAME _____

1) José has 2 ounces of cocaine. If he sells an 8-ball to Antonio for $320 and 2 grams to Juan for $85 per gram, what is the street value of the rest of his hold?

2) Rufus pimps 3 hoes. If the price is $85 per trick, how many tricks per day must each ho turn to support Rufus's $800-per-day crack habit?

3) Jerome wants to cut the pound of cocaine he bought for $40,000 to make 20% profit. How many ounces will he need?

4) Willie gets $400 for a stolen BMW, $100 for stealing a Corvette, and $75 for a 4x4. If he steals 1 BMW, 2 Corvettes, and 3 4x4s, how many more Corvettes must he steal to have $900?

5) Raoul got 6 years for murder; he also got $10,000 for the hit. If his common-law wife spends $100 per month, how much money will be left when he gets out?

6) If an average can of spray-paint covers 22 square feet and the average letter is 3 square feet, how many letters can be sprayed with 3 eight-ounce cans of spray-paint?

7) Hector knocked up 3 girls in the gang. There are 27 girls in his gang. What is the exact percentage of girls Hector knocked up?

8) Bernie is a lookout for the gang. Bernie has a boa constrictor that eats 3 small rats per week at a cost of $5 per rat. If Bernie makes $700 a week as a lookout, how many weeks can he feed the boa with one week's salary?

9) Billy steals Joe's skateboard. As Billy skates away at 35 mph, Joe loads his .357 Magnum. If it takes Joe 20 seconds to load his Magnum, how far away will Billy be when he gets whacked?

Source: Anon

VOCABULARY FROM A WEST-INDIAN MEN'S ROOM

Christopher K. Starr and Mark A. Thomas

In September 1991 one of us (CKS) noticed an extensive series of vocables on a stall wall in a men's washroom at the University of the West Indies (UWI). The series consisted of eight columnar lists of synonyms for various body parts and functions.

The washroom is so situated that it is mainly utilized by staff and students in the Department of Life Sciences. Almost 90% of these students are native to Trinidad and Tobago (UWI administration statistics). There is indirect evidence that members of the technical staff, all native Trinidadians, also contributed to the lists.

One informant estimated that the lists had been initiated about five years earlier, and another confirmed that they were several years old.

Given this background, the lists seemed to us to proffer an unusually complete and unbiased data set. They approximate the sum of vocables representing eight impolite concepts known to educated young men of Trinidad and Tobago.

In order to estimate growth of the lists, for one year beginning 5 September 1991 we recorded at frequent intervals any additions or amendments. In that time 20 vocables were added to the initial 257 (in all quantitative data we disregard repetitions). In the months after we stopped rigorous monitoring, only one novel vocable appeared: "box" was added to list E. Cleaning of the wall has since largely effaced the lists.

The eight lists are presented in the table. Half of the lists appeared to have started just above a heavy line marked across the wall, proceeding upwards, the others starting just below the line and proceeding downwards. As transcribed here, the putative beginning is at the top in each case. Within each list the sequence is only approximately chronological, as some writers inserted new vocables between earlier ones. Additions and amendments are dated in square brackets, in which the month is indicated by a Roman numeral.

Many writers contributed more than once to the lists. Vocables followed by the same superscripted letter or pair of letters appear to have been written by one person, not necessarily all on the same occasion. We infer these connections conservatively, based on idiosyncratic handwriting features.

We adopt as a convenient heading for each list the supposed standard term indicated by one writer (*see* Footnote 1). It is evident from the complete recognition of each of these by all informants that they are indeed a sort of standard.

In order to compare the currency of the terms, we asked three male and three female students—all lifelong residents of Trinidad—to review our transcript of the lists and indicate which they had heard or seen used in the sense given. For each vocable we indicate in the table how many recognized it. Where a vocable was amended, recognition figures are for the original form. On average, the men each recognized 62% and the women 50% of all vocables. A breakdown of these figures by list is given in the table.

Our main purpose here is not to reach conclusions but simply to make available to the maledictology community an exceptionally clean, self-generated data set. We will content ourselves with noting a few points:

1. As expected, vocables were on the whole more familiar to male than female informants. However, the recognition figures for men and women are more similar than we expected. We hypothesize that the differences are more due to

the fact that the data set was male-generated than because young men in Trinidad have more maledicta in their vocabularies. A test will require a comparable female-generated data set, which we have not yet located.

2. A salient feature of list G (*Penis*) is the prominence of weaponry metaphor, while passive terms dominate list E (*Vagina*). Consistent with this is are the many violent terms in list D (*Intercourse*). Comparison of female-generated lists would be especially interesting in this respect.

3. List H (*Homosexual*) seems somewhat enigmatic. Tolerance of homosexuality is low in Trinidad, and overt male homosexuals are rare. This may account for the shortness of the list.

We thank Joanna Chen, Nigel Gomez, Rosemarie Kishore, David Seenath, Jimmy Shah and Suzette Soomai for advice and help in data collecting.

A. **Girlfriend** (n = 32)	Recognition by	
	Men	Women
bone[a] [30.V.1992]	1	0
girlfriend[b, 1]	3	3
client[b]	1	1
skirt[b]	1	0
babe[b]	3	3
chick[b]	3	3
woman[b]	3	3
sweetheart[b]	3	3
half[b] [amended to "better half"]	3	1
dearest[b]	3	3
squeeze[b] [amended to "main squeeze"]	3	3
gul[b] [more standard spelling "gyul"]	3	3
sweets	3	3
wifey	3	3
baby	3	3

A. **Girlfriend** (n = 32) cont'd

	Recognition by Men	Women
'oman [*sic*]	3	3
thing[c]	3	3
item[c]	1	1
ting[c]	3	3
weakness[b, 2]	1	0
strength[b]	0	0
comfort[b]	1	0
worries[b]	1	0
trouble	1	1
sweets	3	3
ball and chain[d] [5.X.1991]	2	0
jamit [4.XI.1991]	3	1
bitch [4.XI.1991]	3	1
flesh[e] [17.III.1992]	1	2
bitch[e] [27.III.1992]	3	1
beast [27.III.1992]	0	1
craft [27.III.1992]	0	1
love [28.IV.1992]	3	3
Mean	2.1	1.8

B. **Cunnilingus** (n = 21)

	Recognition by Men	Women
cunnilingus [f]	3	3
fellatio	3	3
give head	3	2
drink [g]	1	0
ingest	1	0
imbibe	0	0
feast	1	1
munch	1	0
nibble	1	1

B. **Cunnilingus** (n = 21) cont'd

	Recognition by Men	Women
lap up *f*	1	1
chew *f*	0	1
bite	1	0
eat	3	3
lick*h*	3	3
suck*h, 1*	3	3
mouth treatment*i*	0	0
tongue it*i*	2	2
oral*i*	3	3
munch*i*	1	0
jort *g* [slang for "eat"]	1	0
dine *g*	1	0
Mean	1.6	1.2

C. **Bottom** (n = 32)

	Recognition by Men	Women
posterior	3	3
elevation*b*	1	0
bum*b*	3	3
buttocks	3	3
anus	3	3
batee	1	2
bati*b*	1	1
next face	0	0
buns	3	3
rear *j*	3	3
behind *j*	3	3
rectum *j*	3	3
chasee *j*	3	2
bottom*k, 1*	3	3
bumsee*k, 3*	3	2

C. **Bottom** (n = 32) cont'd

	Recognition by Men	Women
batam^k	1	1
ass [not "arse"]	3	3
backside [amended to "backside cat"]	3	3
cacahole	3	2
bumbum	3	2
rump	3	2
fanny	3	3
tail^b	3	3
tailpiece^b	1	0
cheeks ^{l}	3	2
laurel^l [Laurel cars have the largest trunk]	0	0
hump	1	0
seat^m	3	3
butt^m	3	3
bumbulum^b	2	3
gluteus maximus	3	3
tosh [16.XII.1991; more commonly "tush"]	3	2
Mean	2.4	2.2

D. **Intercourse** (n = 68)

	Recognition by Men	Women
give the award [apparently inserted late]	0	0
intercourse ^{j,l}	3	3
sex ^{j} [amended to "sex it" as of 30.V.1992]	3	3
throw down ^{j}	3	1
hit ^{j}	1	0
cover ^{j}	0	0
fick [1.V.1992]	0	0
jam ^{j}	3	3
screw ^{j}	3	3
bull ^{j}	3	3

D. **Intercourse** (n = 68) cont'd	Recognition by	
	Men	Women
fock [j] [amended to "fuck"]	3	3
bang	3	3
pipe [n]	3	1
blaze [n]	2	2
lick-up [n]	3	2
floor [n]	0	1
lay [o]	2	3
lash [o]	1	0
damage [o]	0	1
pierce [o]	0	1
pounce	1	1
beat up	0	1
mate [p]	3	3
penetrate [p]	3	2
copulate [p]	3	2
roast [5.IV.1992]	0	0
thread [p]	1	0
inseminate	3	3
inject	1	1
ride	3	3
interfere	1	1
lick-up [n]	2[4]	2
know [q]	2	2
went into [q]	2	1
invade [r]	1	1
intrude [r]	0	1
crack it [r]	1	0
breed	3	2
mount	3	3
lace	1	1
pump	2	3
plug	1	2
wet	1	0

D. **Intercourse** (n = 68) cont'd	Recognition by	
	Men	Women
molest	3	0
rip	0	0
eat	2	1
buss up	2	2
sleep with	3	3
bed [s]	2	2
puncture [s]	1	0
poison	0	0
full	1	0
enlarge [b]	1	0
widen [b]	1	0
probe [b]	1	1
ram	1	2
apply semen [b]	0	0
sauté [b]	0	0
crack	1	1
open up	1	0
ride [t]	3	2
explode in [t]	2	0
bomb	1	0
quiet	0	0
cool [u]	0	0
soak [u]	0	0
split [t]	2	0
sober [t]	0	0
Mean	1.5	1.2

E. **Vagina** (n = 40)	Recognition by	
	Men	Women
estate	0	0
cunt [j]	3	3

E. **Vagina** (n = 40) cont'd

	Recognition by Men	Women
tun tun [j]	3	3
pussy [j]	3	3
cat [j]	3	3
peggs [j]	0	0
nanny [j]	3	3
vagina [j, l]	3	3
palay [v]	3	3
treasure [v]	1	1
pum pum [Jamaican term]	3	2
slit [b]	3	2
receptacle [b]	2	2
honey	1	1
the girl	0	0
she [w]	0	0
crack	3	1
beaver [25.VI.1992]	2	1
mound	3	3
meow	2	2
hillock	1	0
flesh [x]	3	2
crevice [x]	3	1
hole [x]	3	3
midsection	0	0
sugar walls	3	3
opening	2	1
peehole [y]	0	0
peyahw [y] [possibly a Jamaican term]	0	0
spefhim [possibly a Jamaican term]	0	1
crotch	3	3
punanny	3	2
pit	0	1
front end	1	1
chin rest	2	0

E. **Vagina** (n = 40) cont'd

	Recognition by	
	Men	Women
femininity[z]	3	2
sweetness[z]	2	2
orifice[a, a]	2	2
pokey[a, a]	3	0
burr [possibly "brrr", as in shivering]	0	0
Mean	1.9	1.5

F. **Breasts** (n = 27)

	Recognition by	
	Men	Women
headlights[d] [5.X.1991]	2	0
mammaries	3	2
bouncers	3	1
breadfruits	0	1
silicone	2	1
upper section	2	1
bosom	3	3
milkers[b]	1	0
glands[a, b]	3	1
totties[a, b]	0	0
fruits[b]	1	0
portugals[b] [a citrus fruit]	1	0
melons[b]	3	1
tottots	3	3
top	3	2
chest	3	2
boobies	3	3
boobs	3	3
domes	1	0
jock [3.XII.1991; norm. used for "masturbate"]	0	0
teats	2	2
pair	2	1

F. Breasts (n = 27) cont'd	Recognition by	
	Men	Women
udder	2	2
tits	3	3
breasts [1]	3	3
knockers [1.XI.1991]	3	3
breakfast [a] [20.V.1992]	0	0
Mean	2.0	1.4

G. Penis (n = 41)	Recognition by	
	Men	Women
scud	2	0
boner [a] [26.V.1992]	3	1
penis [a] [26.V.1992]	3	3
toolee [a] [28.V.1992]	3	2
prick [j]	3	3
wood [j]	3	3
tool [j]	3	3
toto [j]	1	1
iron [j]	1	2
penis [j,1]	3	3
gun	1	0
coco	2	1
dung [sic]	0	0
lolo [a, c]	2	2
colo [a, c]	1	1
he [w]	0	0
the boy	2	0
loley [a, c]	2	2
tolee [a, c]	2	2
instrument	1	2
meat	2	1
shaft	3	2

G. **Penis** (n = 41) cont'd	Recognition by	
	Men	Women
bone	3	2
flange	0	0
dick	3	3
wiggy	1	1
manhood	3	2
private	3	3
extension[b]	2	0
organ[b]	3	2
equipment[b]	3	1
package	0	0
tolo[a, c]	1	1
maleness[a, d]	3	2
weapon[a, d]	1	1
ammunition	1	0
six shooter	0	0
phallus	2	2
massive[a, e]	0	1
blessing[a, e]	0	0
monster	1	0
wel [1.XI.1991]	0	0
Mean	1.7	1.3

H. **Homosexual** (n = 16)	Recognition by	
	Men	Women
mick [5.XII.1991]	2	0
homosexual[1]	3	3
gay	3	3
queer	3	3
queen	3	2
bi[b]	3	2
bullerman[b]	3	3

H. **Homosexual** (n = 16)

	Recognition by	
	Men	Women
batiman[b]	2	1
fag	3	3
mantaker[a, f]	1	1
hen[a, f]	3	3
mudpusher	0	0
boysting [i.e. "boy's t'ing"]	2	0
batologist [see "batee" and "bati" in list C]	0	0
acdc	3	2
faggot	3	3
Mean	2.3	1.8

FOOTNOTES

1. Each of these terms (one per list) was circled by the same person. The implication is that these are the standard terms.

2. This and the following three were evidently written by the same person on two different occasions to comprise two couplets, i.e. weakness/strength and comfort/worries.

3. Alternatively "bamsee", as in "[a certain professor] only likes bamsee lickeres" [sic] on the same wall, written by someone who appears not to have contributed to the lists.

4. Why one of our male informants should recognize "lick-up" once and then not recognize it a few seconds later is uncertain. We tentatively assign it to maledicta-fatigue.

In this panel © 2003 by J.C. Duffy of "Fusco Brothers" fame, the cartoonist sneaked a Dutch vulgarity past the "family newspaper" censors. Among the names of card games is **klootzakken**, lit. 'ball-sacks' (scrota), "foolish, stupid, clumsy persons; assholes; dickheads."

Israeli Politicians' Insults

Some of the insults Colette Avital, an Israeli legislator, wants banned from parliamentary debates:

brain defective
degenerate
evil one
eye gouger
fascist
father of violence
filth
gang
government of murderers
gut ripper
humbug
hypocrite
idiot
instigator of murder
Jew-hater
king of the swamp
leech
liar
loathsome
man of blood
may your name be blotted out
mental case

monster
murderer
Nazi
nincompoop
occupying army
parasite
Philistine
pig
P.L.O.
poisoner of wells
poodle
racist
swamp fly
swindler
terrorist
threat to the state
thug
total nonentity
traitor
ugly
venal
worthless

Source: *Harper's Magazine*, March 2002, p. 26. Thanks to Len Ashley.

The Lord's Prayer in Ebonics
Big Daddy's Rap

Yo, Big Daddy upstairs,
You be chillin,
So be yo hood.
You be sayin it, I be doin it
In this here hood and yo's.
Gimme some eats,
And cut me some slack,
Sos I be doin it to dem dat diss me.
Don't be pushing me into no jive,
And keep dem Crips away.
'Cause you always be da Man.
— Aaa-*men*

MODERN SWAHILI
VULVAS AND VAGINAS

Peter Constantine

Swahili street slang of the '90s is a vibrant and colorful linguistic melting pot that has driven many a seasoned lexicographer to despair. If a scholar on a field trip in the streets of Nairobi, Mombasa, Zanzibar City, or even Malindi, should ask: "Excuse me, how do you say 'vagina' in street Swahili?" he will be deluged by a flood of Bantu and non-Bantu words. The melodic string of expressions pouring forth in answer to the question would include ancient and exotic words of Arabic, Hindi, and Persian descent as well as native Bantu words, with occasional Kikuyu, Bemba, and Chinyanya expressions thrown in, not to mention the odd English or English-inspired word favored by the Nairobi or Mombasa high-school crowd.

Among the many synonyms and metaphors for vagina and vulva in Swahili, **koma** and **uke** stand out as the most common, if vulgar, direct references to the organ. Another favorite is the vaguer **utupu**, which in formal Swahili means "nakedness" but has been commandeered by the street crowd as a tasteless allusion to both male and female sexual organs. When one's social setting calls for a more euphemistic reference, the more obscure **uanauke**, "womanhood" or "femininity," is the word of choice.

Other interesting words related to the vagina are **kisimi** and **kinembe**, two tasteless expressions for "clitoris." **Ubikira**, a popular word of Arabic extraction, means "hymen," its Bantu equivalent being **kizinda**, literally "that which makes firm."

The following expressions are generally to be avoided:
Kitabu, "book," is an ancient word of Arabic lineage. As a reference to the vagina it is highly sacrilegious (and in certain circles dangerous): when it was imported into early medieval Swahili, it exclusively meant "Holy Book," as in "The Koran," an association that is still strong in the devoutly Moslem community. It is this very association that prompted the irreverent street crowd to draw the connection, the implication being that the organ, like "The Book," is a mysterious entity that, it is argued, reveals its joyous secrets only to "him who seeks."

Mali, another popular street word of Arabic etymology, means "possessions" or "goods" and is especially favored in circles where a woman's organ is considered to be her "asset." **Mali** is also by extension a crass favorite for "prostitute" and has doubled successfully through the ages as a favorite term for the organ of a well-endowed man.

Mfeleji, also of Arabic provenance, is a modern street pun on **mfeleji wa Suez**, "Suez Canal." Originally witty teenage concoctions, both **mfeleji** and **mfeleji wa Suez** have spilled over into general slang.

Haragwe, "bean," is a word of medieval Persian extraction that from Tanzanian to Southern Somalian Swahili has kept its crisp freshness as a synonym for vagina. The *haragwe* bean's shape, reminiscent of the organ in question, has made it a street favorite.

Ngoma, "drum," belongs to a group of traditional Bantu words that have been reassigned, sacrilegiously according to many, by rougher street elements as a word for vagina. The shape of the drum, and the fact that men "use" it—rhythmically banging away at it—have made it a choice slang word.

Jando comes from the same group of religious Bantu words as **ngoma**. **Jando**, literally "hidden place," is the secret area where religious initiation rites are performed.

Tunda, like **ngoma** and **jando**, was imported from the provinces. It has two meanings and has probably gained popularity on the streets because of the pun in its background. It refers to both the *matunda* fruit and to the bead belt worn by provincial women to cover their pudenda.

Ugali is an old Swahili word of Bantu stock meaning "food." It originally referred only to the traditional porridge paste that is still enjoyed in the provinces. The connection between this tasty paste and a woman's organ is that the vagina, like this staple food, can be said to "satiate" a man's "hunger." (Consider also the more obscure reasoning that porridge, wet and warm, might suggest the tactility of an aroused female organ.)

Kazi, "decoration," is used as a fashionable, if scabrous, synonym for both vagina and food.

Ulimbo, also pronounced **urimbo**, is a popular term inspired by the *ulimbo* trap, a bird trap made of sticky plant sap. This street synonym for vagina professes that women "trap" men with their vaginas. An oft-quoted proverb has it that *Penye urembo ndipo penye uriabo* —"Where there's beauty there's a trap."

Chombo, "cup," but also "apparatus," is a useful expression because it has the double edge of qualifying as a street word for both penis and vagina.

Less pleasant words used only in the roughest and shadiest back alleys are: **Nyufa** and **ufa**, meaning "crack." **Donda** and its insidious derivatives **donda ndugu** and **kidonda**, meaning "ulcer" or "septic sore." **Mchafu** and the closely related **uchafu**, meaning "dirt" or "putrescence."

THEODORE DREISER'S
LITERARY LUST

John McLeish

Theodore Dreiser's second wife, Helen Richardson, used "the most coaxing & grossly enervating [*sic*] words of any girl I know." Dreiser recorded her love talk in Los Angeles on November 11, 1919, in his *Diaries*: "Theo & Helen are between the sheets & no one sees what they are doing. No one, No one. Oh— oh— no one. Theo is between Helens thighs— Helens soft white thighs. Theo is fucking Helens cunt. Yes— he is—yes—yes—oh. Theo is fucking her and Helen is taking it—giving herself to him—her belly—her tittys—her thighs —oh—oh." (*American Diaries 1902–1926*. Philadelphia: University of Pennsylvania Press, 1982, p. 291)

Dreiser also recorded the reaction of his friend Lill to a dictionary of sex terms, in Greenwich Village, on June 6, 1917: "I let her look at new dictionary of venery which just came. She gets excited. Wants to copulate. We do, in back room. Lill leaves." (*Diaries*, p. 165)

The dictionary is Henry N. Cary's *The Slang of Venery*, 1916, which, according to G. Legman's *The Horn Book* (p. 97) is a plagiarism of Farmer and Henley's *Slang and its Analogues* (1890–1904). See Legman's introduction "On Sexual Speech and Slang" to his reprint of volume one of Farmer and Henley (New Hyde Park, N.Y., 1966), p. lxxxiv.

⊗ ⊗ ⊗

Editor's Lament: I have *stacks* of dictionaries of sex terms and a neat back room. Why doesn't a Lillesque woman ever visit *me*?

PORN ACTRESSES
SAY THE DARNDEST THINGS

Kami Andrews *and* Reinhold Aman

In *Maledicta 12*, we had a short collection of wacky utterances by customers overheard and collected by writer Susan Catherine while working as a waitress. In a similar vein, the excerpts below are from a larger collection of snippets from conversations recorded by actress Kami Andrews from her fellow porn actresses, producers, and cameramen. She has an excellent ear for what is hilarious, sad, or just plain goofy.

I corrected some typos and added punctuation marks but otherwise left the material as recorded by Kami on pornography movie sets in 2004 and featured on her racy Website (http://www.kamiland.com). The material below is genuine American lingo, yet you won't find it in academic journals specializing in American speech. It also allows us to peek into the often depressing netherworld of making pornographic films and the concerns of actors, actresses, and producers.

"Fuck me till my ass is bleeding. Blood is nature's lubricant."

A: "I need money for rent."
B: "Go fuck someone."
A: "I can't, football is on."

A: "We should do an inter-racial gardening show called *Spades and Hoes.*"
B: "I don't think the word 'spade' would be well accepted."

"Is my ass bleeding yet?"

"I suck good dick. That's something I can be proud of."

"Isn't that the prettiest asshole you've ever seen?"

"The vibrator slipped lose and got stuck in her ass, and she had to go to the emergency room and have it surgically removed."

"She couldn't take my calls 'cause she has chlamydia."

"Everyone wants to fuck a midget."

"At first I thought you were blaming me, but then I realized you were crazy."

"I can pee on my own face."

"I think someone should give the limo driver a blowjob. He's been so nice."

"October is Syphilis Month!"

"I think the airline stole my drugs."

"I am going to give you an enema, extract it with a turkey baster and feed it to you, OK?"

"My agent didn't tell me there would be fisting. Is the rate the same?"

"Do not grab my cock while I am holding the camera. It's fine to grab it, but not while I'm holding the camera."

Porn actress to a guy with a small dick: "What the hell am I supposed to do with that?"

"You can have all the dildos you can shove in you!"

"It'll be an easy day. He has a small cock."

"Your job is to get the cum out!"

"Her problems come from child molestation. She can't figure out why she wasn't molested. Wasn't she pretty enough?"

"Does blood ever come out of your ass?"

"We thought you looked like shit when you came in, but now that you have make-up on, we want to book another scene."

"I'll suck off anyone that will take me to Carl's Jr." [a fast-food restaurant]

"Leave your shirt off. I don't wanna have to tip the delivery boy."

"Can I lick some coke off your clit…please?"

"What we need here is a stupid little fuck-hole who hasn't yet heard of me and would foolishly agree to come up to my room."

"You are not the first girl to snort cum."

"I made a joke about the smell being her pussy, but it turns out [name] had just been eating fish in the room."

"Um, why is your finger in your butt?"

"Who stole my fucking enemas!?"

"You CAN do double anal!"

"You know if there ain't two dicks in a chick, I just can't be bothered to watch any more."

A: "I am terrified that if I fart I may shit myself."
B: " Oh, my God, me too!"

"I was on set all day and Johnny didn't try to fuck me!"

"I was there for 20 minutes and no one offered me drugs, so I got pissed and left."

"I want a flashlight in my ass too!"

"She isn't even worthy of throat-fucking into submission."

"Her make-up would be perfect if she would just stop five minutes sooner!"

Porn actress: "Oops! I just pooped on your carpet."
Cameraman: "That's why I don't have a dog."

"I am so glad that I have a lifestyle where I can just sit here and masturbate in front of my friends."

"Do you want to eat the cum out of her ass or off her face?"

"I was gonna not do the scene, 'cause I was upstairs and I had one of those 'Oh, my God, this is my life and I am a filthy whore' kinda moments, but once we got fucking, I really got into it."

"Let's give it to her and see if she eats it."

"You can try to fist me if you want."

"Was that blood or lipstick?"

"I wouldn't fuck her if she was dead for like a week."

"We cannot do anything to these girls that their fathers or uncles haven't already done."

"When you see her, be sure and take her to Taco Bell, because that whore needs to eat!!!"

"If you don't swallow, don't bother doing porn."

"She's so white trash. You just can't wash away that much white trash."

"That's not cancer, that's herpes."

"Let me know when you can get two butt plugs in your ass, and I'll let you squirt in my mouth."

"I can't believe you thought five guys peed on you. It was only three!"

"Do you even remember fucking me?"

"Thank you for having a clean ass."

"So we have a black midget with a 9½-inch cock."

Porn actress to producer: "Can I use the bathroom?"
Producer: "Only if I can film it."
Porn actress: "OK."

"Why haven't I sucked your dick yet?"

"Pain is temporary. Film is forever."

"My ass makes me more money than my college degree."

"Oh, we got lots of girls. The problem is we can't find a dog."

"If it makes you feel better: I can fuck chicks I don't want to."

"Who am I again?"

"I'm not used to raping people."

"I accidentally tasted his cum."

"You have to be careful not to cum on her busted-out ass. And whatever you do, don't touch her face."

"How much do you want to just lick the cum off her face?"

"Would you mind eating your own cum?"

"I'm going to pee in the pool. Get the camera!"

"Do you need help stretching out your asshole?"

"I am not going to eat puke out of his asshole!"

"I need to see more tongue actually going in the butt."

"Would you like to see my titties?"

A: "I haven't had a nice poop in two weeks."
B: "You never appreciate your poop till it's gone."

A: "I took the job."
B: "Well, make a doctor's appointment now, 'cause you're going to need it."

A: "Don't use that toilet paper. The good toilet paper is over there."
B: "Good toilet paper?"
A: "Yeah, it sticks to your pussy less."

"Baby, when strangers give you unmarked prescription pills when you first walk in, don't take them."

"By the time the third drug dealer has shown up and left your set, you know the shoot is not going to go well."

"Your ass opened up like a crater. We all looked away, but your friends cheered."

"My dad heard you yelling at the dildo in the kitchen."

"We were done for the scene, but then you guys just started peeing on each other."

"You could really be almost like a real actress."

"OK, you're gonna give the blowjob in the dumpster."

"Wow, your ass is like a big hungry mouth!"

"Honey, don't do [cocaine] lines off the floor. Everyone can see under the [toilet] stall."

"She is your real friend. She hid the toys that you didn't want in your ass."

Richard Freeman, publisher of *BNI* (*Batteries Not Included*, a newsletter featuring politically incorrect notes from the sexual underground), alerted me to Kami's site.

MISCELLANY

American Politicians

After Thornton Rep. Val Vigil had accused Colorado Springs Rep. Bill Cadman of being **"garbage,"** the latter warned his colleague Vigil on the floor of the House: **"If you try that again, I'll ram my fist up your ass."** [*Rocky Mountain News*, Denver, 24 Feb. '05]

Canadian Politicians

In a debate during the 2003 Canadian Election, the then premier of Ontario, Ernie Eves, suggested to Dalton McGuinty, leader of the opposition: "Let's get down to the issues, **you scum-sucking mick pig**, McGuinty." [*The Hammer* 49: "Ontario Election 2003."]

American Indians

Peoria Indians called their neighboring Moinguena Indians *mooyiinkweena* (the source of the Iowa place name *Des Moines*), which means, according to an early French writer, *visage plein d'ordure*, or in plain English, **"shit-face."** William Bright in *Newsletter* XXIII:4 (Jan. 2005, p. 9) of The Society for the Study of the Indigenous Languages of the Americas (SSILA).

Verbal Abuse in Israel

The results of a survey by professors Zvi Izakowitz and Ariela Levenstein of the University of Haifa show that almost one out of five elderly Israelis is exposed to verbal, economic or physical abuse. The study included in-depth interviews with 1,045 urban men and women, average age 74. **The most common form of abuse was verbal abuse—cursing, shouting and threats**—which 14.2% of the elderly faced daily. Women are more abused than men, and Arab women were in the worst position of all, suffering physical violence twice as often as Jewish women. On the other hand, **Jewish men suffered more verbal abuse than Arab men.** [*Ha'aretz* (Israel), 22 Feb. 2005]

German Gypsies

In the USA, activists have been arguing for years whether they should be called "Hispanics" or "Latinos." Now the Gypsies in Germany are arguing about the inscription on a $2.6-million Holocaust memorial in Berlin. The Organization of German Sinti and Roma—the politically correct names for the two groups of Gypsies formerly known as **Zigeuner**, the standard German term meaning "Gypsy/ies"—rejects the planned inscription using the word *Zigeu-*

ner because, they claim, this name is insulting and humiliating to the Sinti and Roma who survived the Holocaust. However, the Sinti Alliance (*Sinti Allianz*) in Cologne insists that the term *Zigeuner* be used. [*Berliner Morgenpost*, 1 March 2005]

Stupid Censor

Among the blasphemies reported by Jeffrey Weiss ("What the *^&%$#@!" in *The Dallas Morning News*, 7 Jan. 2005) is the mild "Holy crap!" When *The Times–News* (Twin Falls, Idaho) reprinted his story on 16 Jan. 2005, some schmuck at that newspaper not only deleted several "offensive" paragraphs (actually, already euphemized to protect tender Texans) but also stupidly censored the writer's "Holy crap!" to "**Holy ----!**", which every reader of that Idahoan paper will, of course, mistakenly interpret as "Holy shit!"

Italian *Culattoni*

After the confirmation of Italy's "anti-gay" Rocco Buttiglione for Justice Commissioner was rejected by the European Parliament in Oct. 2004, Mirko Tremaglia, Minister for Italians Abroad, lamented in a statement issued on official government notepaper that Europe was dominated by **bum boys**: *Povera Europa—i culattoni sono in maggioranza*. ("Poor Europe—the *culattoni* are in the majority."). *The Times* (London, 14 Oct. 2004) explained that the Italian term for "bum boys" derives from *culo*, meaning "arse" or "rump."

Tremaglia, 78, said that he was referring merely to the power of the "gay lobby" in Europe and had translated the term into "plain Italian." "I am an old country boy from Bergamo," he defended himself. "That's how they express themselves in my part of the world." RAI, the Italian state television station, reported the controversy without using *culattoni*, whereas most Italian newspapers had no such inhibitions.

The Austrian newspaper *Der Standard* of 14 Oct. 2004 used the German terms for "gays," **Schwule** and **Schwuchteln**, and the Dutch newspaper *De Volkskrant* of 14? Oct. 2004 was even more specific by explaining that the prestigious Italian Zingarelli dictionary translates *culattoni* as "passive homosexual (vulgar)" but that a more precise translation would be "**kontneuker**" (ass-fucker) or "**rugtuffer**" (back-spitter; one who ejaculates on his partner's back).

U.K. Playground Insults Banned

In March 2005, the British Government circulated a leaflet warning teachers that their pupils' "sexist" terms lead to boys feeling superior to girls and make domestic violence seem more acceptable:

"Sexist language and playground banter that seeks to legitimise violence against women should be challenged." NUT (National Union of Teachers) lists as unacceptable such insults as "**slag**," "**slut**," "**lezzie**," "**pro**," and "**your mum's a whore**."

All sexist insults are to be banned from British playgrounds. Boys should be challenged if they are heard directing such terms at girls. It is considered equally unacceptable for girls to aim such insults at one another. Teachers' leaders said such language is common in secondary schools and even among older children at primaries.

An NUT spokeswoman said: "Words like these promote the attitude that females are lesser beings, and as lesser beings they can become the target of violence. It doesn't have to be physical violence to be mentally destroying. We need to nip that attitude in the bud and get kids to treat each other with respect." [*This is London* (*Evening Standard*) 8 March 2005] *Good luck, lady.*

Teresa Heinz Kerry vs. Ted Kennedy
Before becoming a Democrat, Teresa Heinz Kerry, in her 1975 book *The Power Lovers: An Intimate Look at Politicians and Their Marriages*, angrily called Senator Edward Kennedy a "**perfect bastard**." [*Boston Herald*, 26 July 2004]

Nasty-mouthed Lawyers
Standards of courtesy and behavior among attorneys have been declining to the point that even members of the legal profession find them insufferable. In 2004, the South Carolina Supreme Court took the unusual step of requiring members of the bar to take a one-hour class on civility and then an oath pledging to treat opposing lawyers and clients with "fairness, integrity and civility, not only in court but in all written and oral communications." One incident that spurred the state high court's action involved an attorney taking a deposition who told the witness, "**You are a mean-spirited, vicious witch, and I don't like your face and I don't like your voice**."

State bar associations often complain of incivility among their members. Nasty comments, profanity, lack of cooperation, and raised voices apparently are not unusual in their interactions with each other. At a real-estate closing in Massachusetts, two lawyers got into a fistfight after one called the other a **vulgar name**. In a corporate pollution case, opposing attorneys traded insults like "**fat boy**" and "**Mr. Hairpiece**," interspersed with choice **obscenities**. [*The Chicago Tribune*, 8 March 2005]

Expensive Nobody

In a tiff over a parking space, Giulio C. told a parking attendant: **"Tu non sei nessuno!"** (You are nobody!). Italy's legal system ruled that the seemingly innocuous words constituted slander and fined him 300 Euro ($390) plus 500 Euro legal costs when a court in Trieste turned down his appeal. The court ruled that the phrase *you are nobody* "means precisely *you are a nonentity* and to state that a person is a nonentity is certainly offensive because it is damaging to the dignity of a person."

On the other hand, courts have ruled that the Italian equivalent of "**ball-breaker**" is not slander because although "an undoubtedly rude expression, it is now in common usage." Likewise, "**I'll kick your ass!**" also passes muster because this is a "robust reaction which should be understood in a figurative way." Under Italian law, slander is punishable by a maximum fine of 516 Euro. [Reuters, 9 July 2004]

Boy George vs. Sir Elton John

Sir Elton John was recently badmouthed by fellow gay Boy George: "Elton John is like our headmaster, the **grand old dame of pop,** with a beautiful voice but living in an ornate bubble, full of fresh flowers, surrounded by people who nod and laugh at everything he says, and he doesn't have a sense of humour." [*This is London*, 14 March 2005]

Sir Elton John vs. Taiwanese Journalists

After landing at Taipei's Chiang Kai-Shek airport by private jet to give a concert, Sir Elton John was besieged by photographers and TV crews. News channel ETTV showed Sir Elton clenching his teeth and muttering expletives as he stood with his arms crossed tightly across his chest. "**Rude, vile pigs!**" he shouted. "Do you know what that means? **Rude, vile pigs. That's what all of you are.**" One of the photographers shouted back, "Why don't you get out of Taiwan?" Sir Elton replied, "We'd love to get out of Taiwan if it's full of people like you. **Pig! Pig!**" [*This is London*, 23 Sept. 2004]

Sassy Ann Coulter

Conservative author and lawyer Ann Coulter called Bill Clinton a "**horny hick**" and Hillary "**pond scum**" [*Time*, 18 April 2005, p. 131], Ted Kennedy "**the human dirigible**" [*Time*, 25 April 2005, p. 36], historian Ronald Radosh "**a chickenshit**" [p. 42], and *New York Times* publisher Arthur Sulzberger Jr. "**a little weenie**" [p. 37].

According to Howard Kurtz, during the Clinton impeachment proceedings, Ann Coulter also described Bill Clinton "**creepier and**

slimier than Kennedy.... We're shrugging about this guy using
this woman [Monica Lewinsky] like a dog...."
   Kurtz, a typical Clinton-loving liberal hack, nastily likened "vit-
riolic" Ms. Coulter to a whore: "**The woman on the bar stool—
long blond hair, short black skirt, spiky heels, chain-smoking
Carltons—looks like she's waiting to be picked up.**" [*Washington Post*, 16 Oct. 1998, in Kurtz's column]

Dick Cheney

The Vice President told Sen. Patrick Leahy, who had accused Mr.
Cheney of cronyism, "**Fuck yourself.**" [*Time*, 5 July 2004, p. 15]

Filip Kirkorov

Russian music super-star Filip Kirkorov, who has sold more than
60 million records, was riding high until in a press conference in
the spring of 2004 in Rostov na Donu he destroyed his career by
inexplicably attacking a female journalist. "**I'm irritated by your
pink shirt, your tits and your microphone....**" As Irina Arojan
walked out of the room, he screamed at her, "**Good-bye, cunt!**" Because the Russian word for "cunt," *pizdá*, is far more taboo than its
English equivalent, Kirkorov's outburst caused a huge scandal. [*The
Baltic Times* (Riga), 17–23 Feb. 2005, p. 9]

Jack Abramoff: Another Foulmouthed Liar

Senators at a Senate Indian Affairs Committee hearing called super-
lobbyist Jack Abramoff a "**scumbag**," "**charlatan**," and "**crook**."
He and his partner, public relations executive Michael Scanlon, are
accused of having hoodwinked some $66 million out of their
clients, six Native American tribes.
   E-mails from Abramoff to Scanlon show that Abramoff called his
Indian clients "**morons**," "**monkeys**," "**knuckleheads**," "**losers**,"
"**stupid idiots**," and "**fucking troglodytes**." [*Legal Times*, 5 Oct. '04
and *Albuquerque Journal*, 1 Oct. 2004]
   In Abramoff's sickening, self-serving interview with *Time* magazine, that scumbag lies: "Those regrettable utterances [of which
Time printed only *monkeys* and *losers*] were not directed at my
clients. They were usually reserved for those attacking my clients.
[M]y respect for them is unbounded. The Native Americans I
served are sophisticated business people." [*Time*, 9 May 2005, p. 35]
Right. Can you *believe* the chutzpah of that filthy liar?

Thanks to Brian Chapman, Nathan Say, Carla van der Waal & Vegas Bob

KAKOLOGIA

The Golden Age of Kakologia—the 1970s to the 1990s—is over. Gone are the days when letters and phone calls from alert readers informed me daily of the newest riddles and jokes about the latest disaster, death, or other weirdness happening around the globe. Still, in the past seven years, I've accumulated enough material to fill a book. In this volume I can present just a fraction of the best.

The purpose of "Kakologia" is to record permanently what Americans laughed about during the past decade. Of course, not only Americans joked about the topics and people featured below; riddles, jokes, and illustrations travel quickly around the world these days and, where possible, are translated into other languages and then pop up as "original wit" by foreign imitators of David Letterman and Jay Leno.

Dead Di & Dodi

Within hours of the news that Diana, Princess of Wales, had died on 31 Aug. 1997, together with her lover, Dodi al-Fayed, and their drunk French chauffeur, Henri Paul, the first jokes and comments appeared in the *alt.tasteless.jokes* newsgroup. There was little sympathy for Di and Dodi from the contributors from the U.S., U.K., Ireland, and Australia. One chap wrote: "Too bad the rest of the royal leaches weren't in the back seat." Another, sarcastically: "What was a single mother doing gallivanting with a spoilt-brat philandering playboy in Paris on a Saturday night? Why was she not reading bedtime stories to her boys?" The riddles were of such ferocity as not seen since the "Challenger" explosion. The very first riddle:

What did the French doctors find in Diana's mouth? — *The tip of an Egyptian penis.*

What is Di now? — *A crumpled crumpet.* [*crumpet* = British slang for "woman as a sexual object"]

Why was Di killed? — *It was the wrath of God, for her taking up with a wog.* [*wog* = British slang for a dark-skinned person, such as an East Indian, Pakistani or Arab]

Who is the "Tasteless Photographer of the Year"? — *The first paparazzo on the scene of Di's last drive.*

Which was Di's favorite rock band? — *"The Crash Test Dummies."*

What's the best punishment for paparazzi? — *To use them for live crash test dummies.*

What did Bill Clinton say when he heard of Di's death? — *"Goddamn it! The bitch died on me before I could screw her!"*

How did Di stay so thin? — *It was that crash diet.*

Did you hear that Princess Di was on the radio yesterday? — *Also on the dashboard, the floor, the steering wheel....*

Who was the last guy to fuck Princess Di? — *The French doctor who turned off her life support machine.*

Why will they have to cremate Princess Di? — *Because she won't fit into the coffin—they can't get her to keep her legs closed.*

What's one good thing about Di's crash? — *She won't have to worry about getting her legs blown off by land mines.*

What were Princess Diana's last words to the paparazzi? — *"Will you leave me alone!? I'm a bloody princess!"*

What's the difference between Di and Dodi? — *Di is as dead as Dodi, and Dodi is as dead as a dodo.*

What's worse than being chased by motor bikes? — *Being driven by a drunk chauffeur.*

What was the last thing that went through Dodi's mind? — *The radiator.*

Why is the tunnel's concrete pillar red? — *Because it has Di on it.*

What's the difference between Di alive and Di dead? — *Alive she was full of life; now she's full of embalming fluid.*

How did they get Princess Di's body out of the limo? — *They used royal jelly.*

Why didn't the airbag in the Mercedes-Benz function properly? — *Because he was in the back seat fondling Di.*

What were Di's and Dodi's plans for Saturday night? — *To paint the town red.*

What were Diana's last words to Dodi? — *"You're bleeding on my new dress!"*

What's Burger King's new "Lady Di Combo"? — *Egyptian sausage on an English muffin with ketchup and a bottle of Perrier.*

What's Pizza Hut's new "Princess Di Meatlover's Pizza"? — *It's made with Egyptian sausage and Welsh beaver.*

Why did Di and Dodi drive through the tunnel? — *To get to the other side.*

What did a paparazzo say before chasing them on a motorcycle? — *"I'd kill for a picture!"*

What did Dodi tell the driver? — *"Fuck the speed limit—that's for poor people!"*

Why did the chauffeur speed up to 120 mph? — *He misunderstood Princess Di's moaning in the back seat, "Faster...faster!"*

How did Prince Charles react to the news of Di's accident? — *He was all ears.*

What did the French doctor say to Charles when he picked up the phone? — *"Princess die."*

What did Prince Charles say when he saw the crumpled car? — *"Well, that's the way the Mercedes bends."*

What did Prince Charles, out early walking the dog, reply when a passer-by said, "Morning." — *"No, just walking the dog."*

What happens when you kiss a princess? — *You get killed by a frog.*

What was wrong with Di's driver? — *He had a bad case of tunnel vision.*

What did the French photographer ask Di as she was pulled from the wreck? — *"What will you be wearing at your funeral?"*

What does Lady Di have in common with George Burns? — *They both died when they hit one hundred.*

Versace, Diana, Elton John...two down, one to go.

What will Diana be getting for Christmas? — *The Queen Mother.*

What song did Elton John sing at Dodi's funeral? — *"Goodbye Fellow Prick Dod."*

What's the difference between Elton John and Lady Diana? — *One is composing, the other's decomposing.*

What did Diana really die from? — *Car-pole-tunnel syndrome.*

Where does Di stay when she goes to Paris? — *Any place she can crash.*

What were Di and Dodi drinking before the crash? — *Harvey Wallbangers.*

What do you give the girl who's got everything? — *A seatbelt and an airbag.*

What's the difference between an airbag and an airhead? — *One comes out of the dashboard and the other goes through it.*

What did the French mortuary attendant sing as he was putting the victims of the crash into their body bags? — *"Zip-a-dee Dodi, zip-a-dee Di."*

What did Dodi say to his chaffeur? — *"Do you want to come for a drive with me and Di?"*

Why did Elton John sing at the funeral? — *Because he's the only queen who gives a fuck.*

What will the Queen be giving Fergie for Christmas? — *A trip to Paris, dinner at the Ritz, and a chauffeur-driven Mercedes.*

What did the Queen say when she heard Princess Diana died in a car crash? — *"Was Fergie with her?"*

What was Diana wearing that Saturday night? — *Crushed velvet.*

Why did they cremate Dodi's remains? — *To hide Di's toothmarks on Dodi's dong.*

What do Dodi and the dodo have in common? — *Both are extinct.*

What is the difference between Tiger Woods and Lady Di? — *Tiger Woods has a good driver.*

What do Princess Di and a landmine have in common? — *They're both easy to lay but messy to remove.*

What do the letters DIANA stand for? — *Died In A Nasty Accident.*

What does DODI stand for? — *Died Of Driver Intoxication / Died On Dashboard Impact.*

What's the one thing that attracts Diana more than a wealthy Egyptian? — *A concrete pillar.*

What were Diana's and Mother Teresa's last words? — *"Oh, God! I'm Coming!"*

What was Diana's last complaint? — *"Those photographers drive me up the wall!"*

What does Princess Diana have in common with Hugh Grant? — *They both bought it in the back of a car.*

What's worse than removing red wine from a carpet? — *Removing Di from upholstery.*

What did Di say when the Ritz asked her if she'd like a room for the night? — *"No thanks, I'll just go and crash with my boyfriend."*

What was Henri Paul drinking before he drove the car? — *A Harvey Wallbanger and six chasers.*

Did you hear about the new drink? — *It's called the "Diana Wallbanger."*

What's the difference between paparazzi swarming around Princess Di and flies on shit? — *The flies lose interest once you bury it.*

What's the difference between a Lada and a Mercedes-Benz? — *Princess Di wouldn't be seen dead in a Lada.*

What does a bee have in common with a Mercedes? — *They both make royal jelly.*

Hear about the new Mercedes? — *It comes with two airbags and three bodybags.*

What has 500 legs and 75 teeth? — *The front row at Diana's funeral.*
What's the difference between Lady Di and the East Germans? — *The East Germans survived the wall.*
Why was Lady Di's death a tragedy? — *Because the rest of the Royal Family wasn't in the back of the car with her.*
What's the difference between the London Ritz and the Paris Ritz? — *You get mints after dinner at the London Ritz and minced after dinner at the Paris Ritz.*
Why was the bodyguard so red-faced after the accident? — *Because he had Di all over him.*
What did Diana and Versace have in common? — *They both got screwed by queens and died.*
How many paparazzi does it take to kill Di? — *Fifty: one to drive in front of Di and 49 to take pictures.*
Did the British Secret Service kill Princess Diana? — *No, it was the French underground.*
What have Lady Di and a bottle of French wine got in common? — *The both came from France in a wooden box.*
What vegetable is most like Princess Diana? — *French squash.*
If you go out on the grog, then get in a car with a wog and a frog and drive like a hog, you'll be as dead as a dog.
What is worse than being chased by paparazzi? — *Being chauffeured by a French driver.*
What's worse than being chauffeured by a French driver? — *Being treated by a French doctor.*
Why did Di go to Paris? — *To get smashed!*
What do Diana and a tampon have in common? — *They both go in dark holes and come out red.*
Why didn't Superman come and rescue Princess Diana? — *Because he's a quadriplegic!*

∾

Many posters to the *alt.tasteless.jokes* newsgroup were furious about the above riddles and complained bitterly about others who contributed riddles. Some excerpts, cited verbatim:

▶ I think you are very sick, don't you understand that we have lost one of the worlds greatest people. I am a big fan of Princess Diana, and i was shocked and sickened to find those jokes....

▶ YOU FUCKING SUCK!!!!! I WANT YOU DEAD!!! I WILL PERSONALLY SAW OFF YOUR HEAD WITH A RUSTED CHAINSAW AND SHOVE IT MERRILY UP MY PUS AND SHIT FILLED ASSHOLE....

▶ you sick perverted son of a bitch!!!!!!!!!!! how the hell can you say such rude volger tasteless crap about a women who so loved this world and everyone in it....

▶ hey you asshole, why don't you pick on people like clinton, or bush, or someone like that, princess di was the greatest woman to ever walk on this great earth, people like you aren't fit for a place in hell, and as far as i am concerned you should be shot in the damn head, you communist asshole.

▶ You are a mother fucking son of a bitch you know you asshole, let me know when your mother dies I'll take a picture of you fucking her and then put it on the net, that should be good.

▶ i thought your jokes where clever, but i hope i can think up 160 jokes about your mother when she dies in a car crash.

▶ well even if i don't talke it seriously it still is the dumbest and meanest fucking jokes i've ever heard. i didn't know her personally but it still hurts everyone that reads this and you don't care. you are sick and fucking disgusting people to write about someone like this.

▶ How crude, disrespectful and deranged your jokes are. Never could I imagine anything so inconsiderate being said about such a beautiful person like Princess Diana....

▶ I think it's PATHETIC what you've done!!! Have some respect for the Princess of Whales!!!

▶ really u sick son of a bitch ... i hope u get hit by a truck and die u sorry excuse for a human being ... hey maby they should put u back in that mental institution from which u escaped, the world would be a nicer place to live in....

▶ You are in serious need of an axe in the back of the head. Anyone who can make light of such an awful thing should be picked apart by tree frogs.

▶ HOW DARE YOU!!! What the hell is wrong with you! One of the greatest people this world has ever known and you put these jokes on the internet? You think it's funny? You sick basterd! You are no better than the papparazzi that killed her! I hope you burn in hell for this. You should be shot. No trial, no sentencing, straight to execution! Go to hell!

Iraq War & The Middle East

What's the Iraqi Army motto? — *I came, I saw, Iran.*
What do Miss Muffet and Saddam Hussein have in common? — *They both had Kurds in their way.*
What is the best Iraqi job? — *Foreign ambassador.*

What do Saddam Hussein and General Custer have in common? — *They both wanted to know where the hell all those tomahawks were coming from.*
How do you play Iraqi bingo? — *B-52... F-16... B-2...*
What do you call a first-time offender in Saudi Arabia? — *"Lefty."*
Did you hear about the Muslim strip club? — *It features full facial nudity.*
Why do Palestinians find it convenient to live on the West Bank? — *Because it's just a stone's throw from Israel.*
What has 24 legs and 48 teeth? — *Twelve old Muslim women.*
What does the sign say above the nursery in a Palestinian maternity ward? — LIVE AMMUNITION.
What did the Palestinian girl says to her mommy? — *"After Abdul blows up, can I have his room?"*
What did the Muslim comic say to a patron? — *"Is that a Scud missile under your toga or are you just happy to see me?"*

Men & Women

How do we know God is a man? — *Because if God were a woman, sperm would taste like chocolate.*
If the dove is the bird of peace, what is the bird of true love? — *The swallow.*
What's a blonde's favorite nursery rhyme? — *"Humpme Dumpme."*
Why did God give men a penis? — *So they have at least one way to shut a woman up.*
What's the difference between your paycheck and your dick? — *You don't have to beg a woman to blow your paycheck.*
What's it called when a woman is paralyzed from the waist down? — *Marriage.*
What are the small bumps around a woman's nipples for? — *It's Braille for "Suck here."*
Why are men like laxatives? — *They irritate the shit out of you.*
Why is it so hard for women to find men who are sensitive, caring, and good-looking? — *Because those men already have boyfriends.*
Why did God create man? — *Because a vibrator can't mow the lawn.*
What's the difference between a clitoris and a pub? — *Nine out of 10 men can find a pub.*
What's the definition of "male chauvinist pig"? — *A man who hates every bone in a woman's body except his own.*
Why are women like dog turds? — *The older they get, the easier they are to pick up.*

What's the most active muscle in a woman? — *The penis.*
Why is a pussy like a warm toilet seat? — *They both feel good, but you wonder who's been there before you.*
Why did God create lesbians? — *So feminists couldn't breed.*
How did PMS get its name? — *Because "Mad Cow Disease" had already been used.*

Gianni Versace Murder

On 15 July 1997, gay Andrew Cunanan killed gay Italian fashion designer Gianni Versace in Miami Beach with two bullets to the head.

Why was Versace killed? — *He wanted Cunanan to model for him and asked for two head shots.*
Why did Cunanan shoot Versace? — *Because Gianni was wearing plaids and stripes together.*
How did Versace die? — *He died of a heart attack when he saw that the red from his blood didn't go with the rest of his ensemble.*
What kind of fashion did Versace design? — *Clothes to die for.*
What was Versace's favorite song? — *Nirvana's "Hole in My Head."*
What did *Gianni* Versace's competitors say as he was lowered into the grave? — *"That's the cleanest hole he's been in in years!"*

Michael Kennedy & Sonny Bono

Michael Kennedy, the 39-year-old son of the late Sen. Robert F. Kennedy, was killed on 31 December 1997 by skiing head-on into a tree on Aspen Mountain, Colorado. He hit the tree while videotaping the Kennedy clan playing football on skis with a Nerf (foam rubber) football. According to *The Denver Post* of 3 Jan. 1998, an eyewitness said that the final minutes before the crash were "the most reckless behavior I've ever seen on skis" and "It was the worst time to be doing something like this. Everyone's tired, the snow is getting icy. The conditions alone scared me. It was the stupidest thing I've seen in a long time."

On 5 Jan. 1998, less than a week after Michael Kennedy had skied into a tree, ex-singer and Congressman Sonny Bono slid into a tree at the "Heavenly Ski Resort" near Lake Tahoe, Nevada, also killing himself.

What kind of tree did Michael Kennedy hit? — *A Firhan Firhan.*

What's the difference between John and Michael Kennedy? — *John F. Kennedy:* Profiles in Courage. *Michael Kennedy:* Profile's in Wood.

How rich was Michael Kennedy? — *Immensely. He even had a wood-paneled face.*

Wasn't Michael Kennedy just a rich playboy who did nothing? — *True, but in his final moments he made a big impression.*

How was Michael Kennedy a man of character? — *Even though he cheated on his wife and had sex with a 14-year-old babysitter, in the end, he didn't try to save face.*

Did you hear about Michael's article in *Cosmo* magazine? — *"Skiing Can Be Flattening to Your Face."*

What's the new motto of Kennedy haters? — *"Plant a tree, kill a Kennedy!"*

Why is Michael Kennedy the idol of environmentalists? — *Because he's the ultimate tree hugger.*

From whom did Michael take skiing lessons? — *From the same guy that gave his uncle Ted driving lessons.*

What's the difference between a dog and Michael Kennedy? — *A dog barks a lot and bites; Michael Kennedy bites a lot of bark.*

What's the difference between a golfer and Michael Kennedy? — *A golfer goes whack! ... "Fuck!" and Michael went "Fuck!" ... whack!*

Why don't the Kennedys make good boxers? — *Because they can't take a shot to the head.*

What's one good thing about Michael Kennedy's death? — *His mother, Ethel, didn't have to buy a black dress.*

Where was William Kennedy Smith at the time of the accident? — *At the tree next to Michael's, raping a knot hole.*

What do Sonny and his daughter Chastity have in common? — *He munches a tree, and she munches bush.* [she's a lesbian activist]

Why did Sonny die in a ski accident? — *After being a mayor and a congressman, he wanted to be a Kennedy.*

What preceded Sonny Bono's senseless death? — *Sonny Bono's senseless life.*

How was Bono's body found? — *Sonny side up.*

What did God yell at the Grim Reaper? — *"I said, 'the singer Ono,' not 'Bono'! Dang, this is the second time you botched a job on her!"*

Why are plant biologists amazed about the Michael Kennedy and Sonny Bono deaths? — *Because this is twice in a week that the sap ran into trees.*

What's the newest development in celebrity deaths? — *They used to occur in threes. Now they occur in trees.*
What does "ski" stand for? — *Stops Kennedy Immaturity.*

John F. Kennedy Jr.

During the night of 16 July 1999, John F. Kennedy Jr. (John-John), his wife (Carolyn Bessette) and his wife's sister (Lauren Bessette) were killed when the small airplane he was piloting crashed at sea off the coast of Massachusetts. JFK Jr. was en route to a family wedding on Martha's Vineyard. He was not an experienced pilot and should not have flown, but....

Why didn't JFK Jr. take a shower before leaving for Martha's Vineyard? — *Because he knew he'd be washing up on shore.*
What will they name the movie about JFK Jr.? — *Three Funerals and a Wedding.*
What do the Kennedys miss most about Martha's Vineyard? — *The runway.*
Why was JFK Jr. flying to Martha's Vineyard? — *He wanted to crash his cousin's wedding.*
What does JFK Jr. have in common with a penguin? — *They are both cute and neither one can fly.*
What did JFK Jr. say to his housekeeper before he left? — *"You feed the dogs, I'll feed the fish."*
What do JFK Jr.'s friends call him now? — *"Chum."*
Why was John-John flying that night? — *Because uncle Ted had offered him a ride.*
What's different about this accident? — *The Kennedys used to drown their women one at a time.*
What are the three main causes of death in the U.S. today? — *1. Cancer; 2. Heart disease; 3. Being a member of the Kennedy family.*
Why did Maria Shriver marry Arnold Schwarzenegger? — *To breed bullet-proof, tree-proof, drown-proof Kennedys.*
Where do you find John Kennedy Jr. in the phone book? — *Under "Water."*
What's the difference between Elvis and JFK Jr.? — *Elvis was bloated before he died.*
What was the weather forecast for Cape Cod? — *Cloudy, with widely scattered bodies and debris.*
How is the Coast Guard like a 14-year-old boy? — *Both get excited about finding a wet, crumpled playboy.*

What was the headline in the *National Inquirer*? — *"JFK Jr. goes down on Gay Head. Photos inside."* [Gay Head is a beach on Martha's Vineyard]

Why didn't Superman stop Kennedy's plane from falling out of the sky? — *'Cause he's a quadriplegic!*

What did frustrated St. Peter tell the Grim Reaper? — *"For the last time! I said* TED KENNEDY! *Not Joe, not John, not Robert, not Michael, not Jackie, and not John Jr.! I said* TED!*"*

What will it take to bring the former First Family back together? — *One more bullet.*

What does JFK Jr. and Monica Lewinsky have in common? — *Both went down easily.*

Marv Albert & Mike Tyson

On 12 Feb. 1997, enraged NBC sportscaster Marv Albert (né Marvin Aufrichtig, a German-Jewish name meaning "sincere, candid, honest") viciously bit a woman friend about 18 times on her back and then forced her to engage in fellatio, because she refused to bring another man to their hotel room for a bit of *ménage à trois*. Marv also reputedly wore women's panties and garter belts.

On 28 June 1997, boxer Mike Tyson viciously bit his opponent, Evander Holyfield, on both ears during a heavyweight fight in Las Vegas and then bit off part of one ear.

Why does Marv Albert like going to comedy clubs? — *Because he loves biting humor.*

What did Marv do when he got his pink slip from NBC? — *He put it on.*

What would shyster Johnny Cochran have told Albert's jury? — *"If the panties don't fit, you must acquit."*

What's the difference between Marv Albert and Sharon Stone? — *Marv wears panties.*

Was Marv Albert's back-biting episode all just a misunderstanding? — *When he asked his girlfriend for a blowjob, she said, "Bite me!"*

Why does Marv Albert want to quit his job at NBC? — *Because there is too much backbiting in the office.*

Who was Mike Tyson's trainer? — *Marv Albert.*

Why is Mike Tyson moving to Kansas? — *So he can grow corn and chew all the ears he wants to.*

What is Mike Tyson's favorite Shakespeare quote? — *"Friends, Romans, Countrymen, lend me your ears."*
What's different about Mike Tyson's computer? — *It has two bytes and no memory.*
How does Mike Tyson differ from Metallica? — *Metallica leaves a ringing in your ears; Tyson leaves your ears in a ring.*

World Trade Center

The horrifying destruction of both World Trade Center towers and the airplane crash into the Pentagon on 11 Sept. 2001 left even the most cynical quipsters dumbstruck. Normally, immediately after a well-publicized tragedy or death, riddles are flying fast, but not this time. It took one week until I heard the first and only one (the first one below), and then silence, eerie silence. No e-mails, no letters, no phone calls with wisecracks, as is normally the case. The horror was simply too much. The jokes and riddles after the first one were gathered by Tom S. from the *alt.tasteless.jokes* newsgroup.

Who are the fastest readers in the world? — *New Yorkers. Some of them go through 110 stories in five seconds.*
Why do tourists flock to New York? — *Because it's a blast.*
What three seating areas did the World Trade Center restaurant offer? — *Smoking, Non-smoking, and Burned-beyond-recognition.*
What's the world's most efficient airline? — *American Airlines: Leave Boston at 7:59. Be in your office in New York City at 8:45.*
What was the last thing going through Mr. Smith's head in his 90th-floor office of the WTC? — *The 91st floor.*
Why are police- and firemen New York's finest? — *Because now you can run them through a sieve.*
What's the Number One drink served on American Airlines? — *Flaming Manhattan.*
What's the difference between the attack on New York City and the Oklahoma City Bombing? — *Again foreigners prove they can do it better and more efficiently.*
What does WTC stand for? — *What Trade Center?*
Famous last words: *"Amal, was this tower here yesterday?"*
NEWSFLASH... The WTC has been destroyed... Thousands of New York executives feared dead... Hookers all across the city are in mourning....

"It's a bird!" —"It's a plane!" — "It's ... Oh fuck, it *is* a plane!"
New York, New York, so good they hit it twice.
How many sides to a Pentagon? — *Four.*

Michael Jackson

What does Michael Jackson call a school bus? — *"Meals on wheels."*
What does Michael Jackson never say after having sex? — *"Why don't you grow up?"*
What did Michael Jackson tell the priest? — *"Hey, I saw him first!"*
Do you know when it's bed time at Michael Jackson's house? — *When the big hand is on the little gland* [or: *hand*].
What did Michael really mean when he said he likes "38-year-olds"? — *Thirty 8-year-olds.*
What's a McJackson sandwich? — *It's 46-year-old meat between 13-year-old buns.*
Under which new law was Michael Jackson charged? — *Three tykes and you're out.*
What do Michael Jackson and whiskey have in common? — *They both come in small tots.*
Why did Michael Jackson rush over to Wal-Mart? — *He heard that little boys' underpants were half off.*
What's soft, warm, brown and found in a boy's underpants? — *Michael Jackson's hand.*
What's the difference between a supermarket bag and Michael Jackson? — *One is white, made of plastic and should be kept away from children. The other is used to carry groceries.*
What does Michael Jackson describe as a "perfect ten"? — *Two five-year-olds.*
How do you know Michael has a hot date? — *When a tricycle is parked in the driveway.*
What do Michael Jackson and a jockey have in common? — *They both ride three-year-olds.*
What did Michael Jackson say the first time he saw his son? — *"That's mine? How come he looks like a nigger?"*

Concorde Crash

On 25 July 2000, an Air France Concorde jet bound for New York crashed in a ball of fire shortly after take-off in Paris, killing 113 people—100 passengers (most of them Germans), nine crew members, and four on the ground—when the aircraft hit the Hotelissimo hotel. Interestingly, the only riddles came from English contributors, reflecting the Brits' habitual gibes at the "Huns" and "Frogs."

The first set of riddles I received were composed by Alan Roberts, a British comedy writer.

Air France: Killing More Germans Than the Autobahn.

What, if anything, does the Concorde crash prove? — *God is Jewish.*

Why do rich people fly the Concorde? — *They have money to burn.*

What's the most tragic thing about the Concorde crash? — *99.9% of the German population is still around.*

What was the pilot's final announcement? — *"Relax, you'll be in your hotel room before you know what hit you."*

Why was the Concorde named after a grape? — *Throw it against a building and it splats.*

What's the difference between the two? — *The grape: Merlot. The plane: Too low.*

What's Steven Spielberg's next film? — *"Life is Not Beautiful, But This Helps."*

The second batch of riddles came from P., who received them from his daughter in England:

Why do affluent German tourists choose to fly Concorde? — *Because they'd not be seen dead on anything else.*

How do you fit 100 Germans into a small French hotel? — *On Concorde!*

What's the new express service offered by Air France? — *It guarantees you can be off your plane and in your hotel in all of two minutes.*

Why is the Concorde such good value for money? — *You get the hotel thrown in.*

The French killed more Germans on Tuesday than in two World Wars.

So many German tourists. So few Concordes.

The Clintons & Monica Lewinsky

What did Al Gore say after the Lewinsky story broke? — *"Why do they call* me *the stiff man in the White House?"*

What position did Monica Lewinsky have at the White House? — *The missionary position.*

What's the latest Clinton dodge? — *"I didn't impale."*

Why does Clinton wear underpants? — *To keep his ankles warm.*

What's the difference between Monica Lewinsky and the Titanic? — *The Titanic went down only once.*

What's the difference between Bill Clinton and the Titanic? — *Only 200 women went down on the Titanic.*

What does Bill Clinton say to Hillary after sex? — *"I'll be home in 20 minutes, dear!"*

What's the first thing Bill said after the Lewinsky allegations? — *"She never* could *keep her mouth shut."*

What's the difference between President Kennedy and President Clinton? — *In Kennedy's time, we had Camelot; in Clinton's, we have Came-a-lot.*

What's Monica Lewinsky's new television show? — *"Eat the Prez."*

What are the Secret Service's new code names for Slick Willie? — *"PokeHerface" and "Unabanger."*

What's Hillary's new book? — *It Takes a Village to Satisfy My Husband.*

What book is Bill working on? — *The Heartbreak of Satyriasis.*

What was Bill Clinton's biggest mistake? — *He didn't have Ted Kennedy drive Monica home.*

What does Ted Kennedy have that President Clinton wishes he had? — *A dead girlfriend.*

What advice did Yasir Arafat give Clinton? — *"Goats, Bill, goats. They don't talk."*

What do Bill Clinton and Ross Perot have in common? — *They both heard a giant sucking sound.*

What do Monica Lewinsky and Bob Dole have in common? — *They were both upset when Bill finished first.*

What is Bill's definition of safe sex? — *When Hillary is out of town.*

What did Clinton ask Monica? — *"How would you like to be on the President's staff?"*

What instrument did Monica play in high school? — *The skin flute.*

What do rollerbladers and Monica have in common? — *They both need to wear kneepads.*

What do Nicole Simpson and Monica have in common? — *They both have stains on their dresses.*

What do you get when you cross Monica Lewinsky with Mike Tyson? — *Clinton's worst nightmare.*

What was Hillary's first reaction to the scandal? — *She was gonna cut his balls off but then remembered that she was wearing them.*

Who's Hillary's choice for the next White House intern? — *Lorena Bobbitt.*

What game did Bill Clinton want Paula Jones to play? — *"Swallow the leader."*

When did Clinton realize that Paula Jones wasn't a Democrat? — *When she didn't swallow everything he presented.*

What did Clinton say when he heard that Paula Jones was speaking to the press? — *"Now she opens her mouth!"*

What's the similarity between Bill Clinton and a carpenter? — *One screw in the wrong place and the whole cabinet falls apart.*

What do Clinton and Nixon have in common? — *A deep throat brought down both their presidencies.*

What did Bill Clinton say when asked about Ruanda? — *"I did not have sexual relations with that woman."*

Which of the White House interns is the head intern? — *The one with the dirty knees.*

What's Bill Clinton's definition of protected sex? — *Secret Service agents posted outside the door.*

What's the difference between the Clinton White House and a whorehouse? — *You have to pay for sex in a whorehouse.*

How is Bill Clinton like a railroad track? — *He's been laid all over the country.*

What's the best thing about being a female White House intern? — *All of the "hands on" experience.*

Should we feel sorry for Monica? — *No, she'll be back on her knees in no time.*

How did Bill reply to questions about coaching Monica's testimony? — *"It wasn't words I put in her mouth."*

What was inside a hidden pocket in Monica's dress? — *A big wad of bills.*

How is Monica Lewinsky like a vending machine? — *You insert a bill in both.*

Was Monica lying? — *No, she was on her knees.*

Why does Chelsea have no brothers and sisters? — *Because Monica swallowed them all.*

What do Bill Clinton and JFK have in common? — *Both ended their presidencies by staining a woman's dress.*

What's special about Wrigley's new chewing gum called "Lewinsky"? — *It's guaranteed to blow a Bubba.*

Why couldn't Monica auction off her blue dress? — *Because the President put a deposit on it.*

What's the difference between Monica's blue dress and Bill Clinton? — *The blue dress will eventually come clean.*

What's a good punishment for Clinton? — *Overdose him on Viagra and lock him in a room with Janet Reno.*

How does Bill describe sex with Hillary? — *"Close, but no cigar."*

Why was President Clinton so afraid of Monica Lewinsky's testimony before Senators and House prosecutors? — *He was afraid she might cough up some new evidence.*

What's the difference between the Queen of England and the President of the U.S.? — *You have to go down on only one knee in front of the Queen.*

How can you tell Bill Clinton is insane? — *He has a Gentile Lawyer and a Jewish Mistress.*

What's the fluid capacity of Monica Lewinsky's mouth? — *One* U.S. *leader.*

Why are Monica Lewinsky's cheeks so puffy? — *Because she's withholding evidence.*

How are Paula Jones, Hillary Clinton, Gennifer Flowers, and Monica Lewinsky alike? — *To take them home, you need three paper bags: one for her head, one for your head, and one for your dog's head so he'll respect you in the morning.*

What will Bill Clinton do after Hillary is dead? — *Lay Flowers on her grave every chance he gets.*

Why does Hillary Clinton converse with the spirit of Eleanor Roosevelt? — *Because Eleanor was the only other icy lesbian First Lady.*

What's the difference between Hillary and a refrigerator? — *It's warmer in the refrigerator.*

> JFK: "Ich bin ein Berliner!"
> Nixon: "I am not a crook."
> Reagan: "Tear down that wall, Mr. Gorbachev."
> Bush: "Read my lips."
> Clinton: "Suck my dick."

Johnny Cochran's closing arguments for Bill Clinton:
— *If the dress ain't a mess, he won't need to confess.*
— *If she's not spread-eagle, then it's not illegal.*
— *If the sex is just oral, it's not really immoral.*
— *If she's only eatin', it sho' ain't no cheatin'.*
— *If the bitch didn't spit, you've go to acquit.*

Hillary and Chelsea are having a mother/daughter talk. Hillary asks Chelsea, "You have been going to college for a while now. Have you had sex yet?" — "Well, not according to dad."

Monica walks into her dry-cleaning store and tells the guy, "I've got another dress for you to clean." Slightly hard of hearing, the clerk asks, "Come again?" — "No," says Monica, "this time it's mustard."

There once was a gal named Lewinsky
Who played on a flute like Stravinsky.
   'Twas "Hail to the Chief"
   On this flute made of beef
That stole the front page from Kaczynski.

Said Bill Clinton to young Ms. Lewinsky,
"We don't want to leave clues like Kaczynski.
   Since you look such a mess,
   Use the hem of your dress
And wipe that stuff off of your chinsky."

Thanks to George Schultz, Feargal Murphy, John McGrath, David Pressman, Lou Boxer, Patrick Kearney, Tom Slone, Charles Collins, David Broome, Janice Terry, and other contributors to "Kakologia."

"What if I was to give you a choice, Lisa.... I can say I'm sorry for being insensitive to your needs and not taking your feelings about our relationship seriously, whereupon we make up and possibly even conclude the discussion with lovemaking ... or I could just take a .357 magnum and paint the wall with your spoiled-little-white-bitch brains." —*Unknown artist, 1997*

THE SCHITT CLAN HISTORY

How many times has someone said to you during a heated argument, "You don't know jack shit!"—a common American exclamation meaning "you don't know anything"? Now you will learn the entire story.

Jack Schitt is the sole son of **O. Schitt**, the manure magnate, and **Awe Schitt**, keeper of the "Knee-Deep Inn" located near the headwaters of Schitt Creek and known for its hard stools and cow pies. The high point of his newspaper career came in China when he interviewed Chairman Dung. He then moved on to Japan where he married the famous Japanese actress **Noh Schitt** and was awarded the Ordure of Merit Turd Class for his research on coprolites.

Sadly, **Holy Schitt**, the first of their six little Schitts, passed on just after birth. Next came twin sons, **Deep Schitt** and **Dip Schitt**, followed by two girls, **Fulla Schitt** and **Giva Schitt**, and by another son, **Bull Schitt**.

For the sake of family tradition, **Bull Schitt** took over the hole Schitt Works his granddad had established. But, alas, **Bull** was gay and got AIDS from his Peruvian pal, Guano, which left him too pooped to work, so vice president Pierre LaTrine, took over.

In the meantime, **Dip Schitt** married **Dumb Schitt**, a high-school dropout. **Deep Schitt** married **Lotta Schitt**, who bore him a timid son, **Chicken Schitt**, and an aggressive son, **Tuff Schitt**.

Fulla Schitt and **Giva Schitt** married the Happens brothers. The **Schitt-Happens** children are **Dawg Schitt**, **Byrd Schitt**, and **Horace Schitt**. **Deep Schitt**, after a troublesome divorce, married a spicy Italian who became **Pisa Schitt**, and they are now expecting their twins, **Little Schitt** and **Baby Schitt**.

Now you know Jack Schitt and his extended family. So, next time someone says, "You don't know Jack Schitt!" you can reply "Horse Apples! Don't be fecesious. I not only know Jack Schitt butt the hole family as well."

Thanks to Leonard Lewis and many others

BIBLIOGRAPHY

Alexander, Richard J. **Aspects of Verbal Humour in English.** Tübingen: Gunter Narr Verlag, 1997. 217 pp.

Ashley, Leonard R. N. **The Dictionary of Sex Slang.** Fort Lee, N.J.: Barricade Books. In preparation for late 2005.

Bosmans, Bart and Axel Thiel. **Guide to Graffiti-Research.** Gent: Uitgeverij Rhinoceros, 1995. 313 pp.

Claire, Elizabeth. **Dangerous English 2000! An Indispensable Guide for Language Learners and Others.** McHenry, Ill.: Delta Publ. Co., 1998. 202 pp., 3rd ed.

Cornog, Martha. **The Big Book of Masturbation: From Angst to Zeal.** San Francisco: Down There Press, 2003. 335 pp.

Dagrin, Bengt. **Stora Fula Ordboken.** Stockholm: Carlsson, 2000. 503 pp. [Paperback, 7,000 words, 50 SEK, €5.50 or US$5.00. Order from B.D., Österportstorg 5-A, S-271 41 Ystad, Sweden]

Dalzell, Tom. **Flappers 2 Rappers: American Youth Slang.** Springfield, Mass.: Merriam–Webster, 1996. 256 pp.

___. **The Slang of Sin.** Springfield, Mass.: Merriam–Webster, 1998. 385 pp.

Drummond, D.A. and Gareth Perkins. **Dictionary of Russian Obscenities.** Oakland, Calif.: Scythian Books, 1987. 11th printing, 1996. 94 pp.

Grassi, Natascia. **La traduzione degli insulti nel doppiaggio di film americani.** Thesis, Università di Bologna, 2003. (On the [mis-]translations of insults in American films dubbed into Italian; plus detailed discussion of insults, curses, swearwords)

Green, Jonathon. **The Big Book of Being Rude: 7000 Slang Insults.** London: Cassell, 2000. 380 pp.

___. **The Big Book of Bodily Functions: 4500 Words for Bodily Functions and Body Parts.** London: Cassell, 2002. 352 pp.

___. **The Big Book of Filth: 6500 Sex Slang Words and Phrases.** London: Cassell, 1999. 288 pp.

___. **Cassell Dictionary of Insulting Quotations.** London: Cassell, 1998. 288 pp.

___. **Cassell's Dictionary of Slang.** London: Cassell, 1998. 1316 pp.

___. **Cassell's Rhyming Slang.** London: Cassell, 2000. 255 pp.

Gregersen, Edgar A. **1001 Insults in 200 Languages: Your Mother's Testicles, Your Grandfather's Mouth, and Other Maledictions.** New York: Irvington, forthcoming (2005).

Guri, Yosef. **Lomir hern gute psures: yidishe brokhes un kloles** [Let's Hear Only Good News: Yiddish Blessings and Curses. In Yiddish, Hebrew, English, Russian]. Jerusalem: The Hebrew University Magnes Press, 2004. 280 pp.

Havryliv, Oksana. **Pejorative Lexik: Untersuchungen zu ihrem semantischen und kommunikativ-pragmatischen Aspekt am Beispiel moderner deutschsprachiger, besonders österreichischer Literatur.** Frankfurt am Main: Peter Lang, 2003. 155 pp.

Jay, Timothy. **Why We Curse: A Neuro-Psycho-Social Theory of Speech.** Philadelphia/Amsterdam: John Benjamins, 1999. 328 pp.

Jenstad, Tor Erik. **Den store norske skjellsordboka**. Oslo: Marcus For-
lag, 1992. 192 pp.
___. **Nye skjellsordboka**. Trondheim: Tapir Forlag, 1999. 159 pp.
Kiełbasa, Stanisław [pseud.]. **Dictionary of Polish Obscenities**. Oakland,
Calif.: Scythian Books, 3rd rev. ed. 1994. 93 pp.
Masthay, Carl. **Kaskaskia Illinois-to-French Dictionary**. St. Louis: Carl
Masthay, 2002. 757 pp. Chapter of Kaskaskia maledicta, pp. 35-39. (Or-
der from C.M., 838 Larkin Ave., St. Louis, MO 63141–7758)
Matisoff, James A. **Blessings, Curses, Hopes, and Fears: Psycho-Osten-
sive Expressions in Yiddish.** Stanford: Stanford University Press, 2000.
2nd ed., with a new preface and updated bibliography, xxxi + 160 pp.
Montagu, Ashley. **The Anatomy of Swearing**. Philadelphia: Univ. of
Pennsylvania Press, 2001. 370 pp. Reprint of the original 1967 edition.
Nežmah, Bernard. **Kletvice in psovke**. Ljubljana: Nova revija, 1997. 182
pp. (Slovenian cursing and swearing)
Palmer, Joe Darwin. **Watch Boys and Other Stories: A Collection of
Biographical and Fictionalized Stories and Personal Essays About
Islamic, Thai, and American Culture**. Cranston, R.I.: The Writers'
Collective, 2003. 329 pp. (Not maledictive, but fascinating.)
Paros, Lawrence. **Bawdy Language: Everything You Always Wanted to
Do But Were Afraid to Say**. Kirkland, WA: Kvetch Press, 2003. 264 pp.
Pfeiffer, Herbert. **Das große Schimpfwörterbuch: Über 10.000
Schimpf-, Spott- und Neckwörter zur Bezeichnung von Personen**.
Frankfurt am Main: Eichborn, 1996. 557 pp.
Raeithel, Gerd. **Der ethnische Witz. Am Beispiel Nordamerikas**. Frank-
furt am Main: Eichborn, 1996. 192 pp.
Sanders, Ewoud and Rob Tempelaars. **Krijg de vinkentering! 1001 Ne-
derlandse en Vlaamse verwensingen**. Amsterdam/Antwerp: Uitgeverij
Contact, 1998. 192 pp.
Siegl, Norbert. **Graffiti-Enzyklopädie: Von Kyselak bis HipHop-Jam**.
Wien: Österreichischer Kunst- und Kulturverlag, 2001. 256 pp.
Slone, Thomas H. **Prokem: An Analysis of a Jakartan Slang**. Oakland,
CA: Masalai Press, 2003. 98 pp.
___. **Rasta is Cuss: A Dictionary of Rastafarian Cursing**. Oakland, CA:
Masalai Press, 2003. 98 pp.
___. **One Thousand One Papua New Guinean Nights: Folktales from
Wantok Newspaper**. Oakland, CA: Masalai Press, 2001. Two volumes,
528 + 613 pp. (1,047 folktales originally published between 1972 and 1997
in Tok Pisin [Pidgin English]. Translated into English; various indices.
Not maledictive, but fascinating.)
van Sterkenburg, Piet G.J. **Vloeken: Een cultuurbepaalde reactie op
woede, irritatie en frustratie**. Den Haag: Sdu Uitgeverij, 2001. 715 pp.
Wang, James J. **Outrageous Chinese: A Guide to Chinese Street Lan-
guage**. San Francisco: China Books, 1994. 126 pp.
Weihs, Richard. **Wiener Wut: Das Schimpfwörterbuch**. Wien: Uhudla
Edition, 2000. 90 pp.
Zhelvis, Vladimir I. **Pole Brani**. Moscow: Ladomir, 1997. 331 pp. (The
Field of Swearing: Swearing as a Social Problem)
Zhou, Yimin and James J. Wang. **Mutant Mandarin: A Guide to New
Chinese Slang**. San Francisco: China Books, 1995. 170 pp.

CONTRIBUTORS

Reinhold Aman earned a Ph.D. in Medieval Literature and Germanic Philology from the University of Texas in 1968. He edits, typesets, publishes, and ships MAL to 78 countries and has lectured on Verbal Aggression in the USA, Canada, Europe, and South America. More information in earlier volumes and at **http://www.sonic.net/maledicta/**.

Kami Andrews is a model and actress and appears mainly in XXX-rated films. She lives in Pennsylvania.

Hugh Clary is a pseudonym of Henry Hurst, founder of Pegasus Air Express, Inc., an independent airfreight forwarder based at BWI Airport in Baltimore, MD. Now retired and living in Albuquerque, NM, he enjoys a regular schedule of chess, tennis, and bridge, as well as posting limericks and other light verse on various Usenet forums.

Peter Constantine is the author of books on Far Eastern languages, including *Japanese Slang: Uncensored, Japan's Sex Trade: A Journey Through Japan's Erotic Subcultures, Making Out in Indonesian,* and *Making Out in Korean*. He is currently translating novels from Russian, Modern Greek, Albanian, and German.

Edgar A. Gregersen, Professor Emeritus of Anthropology, Queens College and Graduate School CUNY, Ph.D. Yale University, is the author of *The World of Human Sexuality* (New York: Irvington) and *1001 Insults in 200 Languages: Your Mother's Testicles, Your Grandfather's Mouth, and Other Maledictions* (a cross-cultural study), to appear in 2005.

Helena Halmari is an Associate Professor of English at Sam Houston State University, Huntsville, Texas. She received her Ph.D. in Linguistics from the University of Southern California in 1994. Dr. Halmari has taught Linguistics at the University of Florida, Rice University, and the University of California in San Diego. Before moving to the United States, she taught high school English and Russian in Finland.

John McLeish lives in Glasgow, Scotland.

Bruce Moore has a Ph.D. from the University of New South Wales. His main research interests are Old and Middle English Literature and currently the development of the Australian language in the 19th century. Formerly at the Australian Defence Force Academy, he is now affiliated with the Australian National Dictionary Centre in Canberra.

Joe Darwin Palmer, Ph.D. 1969 in English Language and Literature, University of Michigan, is curator of the Loyalist Pine Cottage in Abercorn, Québec, where he reads and writes as much as he can. Professor

Emeritus Palmer also taught applied linguistics in many universities in Asia and Africa, ending at Concordia University in Montréal. He is a rare American with dual Canadian citizenship.

Ken Pontac was born in Glendale, Calif., in 1957. Since 1978 he has produced animated cartoons for television, including the ABC Saturday morning show "Bump in the Night." Mr. Pontac lives near San Francisco with his lovely wife Susan and their pet rats.

David W. Porter received the doctoral degree from the University of Texas at Austin, where he studied language and literature. He has taught English in Japan, Egypt, and the United States, and is now Professor of English at Southern University, Baton Rouge, Louisiana. His most recent publication is *Excerptiones de Prisciano, The Excerpts from Priscian (Anglo-Saxon Texts* 4).

Joseph S. Salemi holds a Ph.D. in Renaissance literature from New York University. He has published translations from Greek, Roman, and Provençal poets in more than 70 journals. His critical articles have appeared in *Chaucer Review, Allegorica, Blake Quarterly, Classical and Modern Literature*, and elsewhere. He teaches at New York University and Hunter College, CUNY. Dr. Salemi's latest book of poems, *Masquerade*, was published by Pivot Press, Brooklyn, in 2005.

Christopher K. Starr did his graduate degrees at the Universities of Kansas and Georgia. Since then, he has worked in Canada, the Philippines, Taiwan, Trinidad, and the USA. His professional scholarly interests are in the behavioral ecology of land invertebrates and the history of biology, with a serious side-interest in folklore. Dr. Starr teaches now at the Trinidad campus of the University of the West Indies.

Mark A. Thomas earned his graduate degrees at the Trinidad campus of the University of the West Indies and at St Andrew's University. He is now on staff at the Jamaica campus of the University of the West Indies, where his research is in vertebrate physiology.

Carla van der Waal studied Dutch and Fine Arts. She lives in Utrecht, The Netherlands. Her interests are other cultures and languages, cooking and traveling.

Vladimir I. Zhelvis, born in 1931 in Leningrad, is an Associate Professor of English Philology at the Pedagogical Institute in Yaroslavl, Russia. His Cyrillic name is also transliterated as Želvis, Jelvys, etc. More about Dr. Zhelvis in *Maledicta 10*.

☞ ☞ ☞

Osmond Beckwith
Vernon: An Anecdotal Novel

Breaking Point, 1981. 195 pp. Illustrated by Michael McCurdy.
ISBN 0-917020-02-7 • $10

As the subtitle indicates, this first novel by a writer of short fiction consists of episodes in the life of a farm boy, Robert Parsons, from first memories through sexual awakening, in and around the fictional country town of Vernon during the Twenties and Thirties. However, both time and setting are purposely vague in comparison to the intensely and minutely detailed perceptions and emotions that Robert feels during the course of a normal childhood. Beckwith uncannily evokes the mind of a child rationalizing the strange ways of an adult world and coping with the changes in his own body and capabilities. McCurdy's stark woodcuts give an aura of added significance. An interesting experiment in the psychological novel, beautifully designed and printed. — *Shelly Cox, Special Collections, Southern Illinois University Library, Carbondale.*

In addition to the Shelly Cox review above, *Vernon* has been praised by G. Legman, X. J. Kennedy, Piers Anthony and other authors.

Readers with a USA address are invited to ask for a free copy (free except for $2 shipping) of Mr. Beckwith's novel *Vernon.*
Please mail your request to:
Osmond Beckwith, 376 Franklin Road, Denville, NJ 07834

By an unknown artist